In The FOOTSTEPS *of the* MAGI

A PILGRIMAGE FOR PEACE FOR JESUS' 2000TH BIRTHDAY

Robin Wainwright
209 - 743 - 6493

ROBIN CATLIN WAINWRIGHT

Printed in the United States of America.

Library of Congress Control Number: 2022936185

ISBN   Paperback   978-1-68536-470-0
            Hardback   978-1-68536-471-7
            eBook   978-1-68536-472-4

Westwood Books Publishing LLC
Atlanta Financial Center
3343 Peachtree Rd NE Ste 145-725
Atlanta, GA 30326

www.westwoodbookspublishing.com

To my wife, Nancy, who went with me to
every country, and over every mile

Part One

PREPARING FOR THE IMPOSSIBLE 1992 TO 2000

CHAPTER ONE

COMING UP WITH A WILD IDEA

My wife Nancy and I came up with this wild—probably impossible—idea. We wanted to organize an International Pilgrimage that would travel on foot and by camel, following the route of the original Magi through Iran, Iraq, Syria, Jordan and Palestine, to arrive in Bethlehem on Christmas Day, 2000, to honor Jesus on His 2000th birthday. It might be impossible--but wouldn't it be wonderful if somehow we could actually do this?

So where did our wild and probably impossible idea come from? I suppose it began in the fall of 1992. I was committed to attend a conference in Nicosia, Cyprus, with Evangelicals for Middle East Understanding (EMEU) and the Middle East Council of Churches (MECC) in early October of 1992. This would be the first historic formal interaction of American Evangelicals with MECC. Following the conference, some of the American participants were planning to travel to Israel and Palestine for a tour of the Holy Land. My soon-to-be wife Nancy and I were planning to get married that fall, and had not yet settled on where this should take place. So because of the timing of EMEU/MECC conference and the Holy Land tour to follow, we decided that we should try to get married in Bethlehem!

So it was that on September 28th, 1992, I traveled to Miami, Florida, to meet with Nancy at her mother's home. Nancy's father, Willard Ware, had died in 1984 and her mother, Rhoda Ware, had soldiered on as the strong-willed Matriarch of the family. I was about to discover exactly what that meant. On the morning of September 30th Nancy's mother woke me up in the library, and Nancy from her upstairs bedroom, and informed us that we had to get up right away and go down to the Clerk of the Court's office to secure a marriage license. She was concerned that our marriage in Bethlehem might not be legal, so to be on the safe side she had arranged for the Pastor of her local church to come to her house that afternoon and marry us!

I guess in the old days this is what they might have called a "shotgun" wedding, but since both Nancy and I were eager to marry anyway, we didn't argue. By that afternoon we were standing there in the living room and sharing our wedding vows, with her mother's maid and handyman as witnesses.

The only problem was that I was due to depart immediately to catch a plane, in order to attend an earlier conference at the same hotel in Cyprus sponsored by Zwemer Institute. So I only had 20 minutes to kiss my new bride and say goodbye to my new mother-in-law, before rushing off to the Miami airport to catch a plane to Atlanta.

Thank goodness I got to Atlanta in time to get on the plane that was heading to Cyprus. But as I was sitting on the plane reading the daily paper while waiting to depart, the stewardess came walking down the isle to pass on to me an important message: "Your wife is outside asking for the keys to the rental car". What? What wife? I didn't have a wife in Atlanta! Then I remembered that a couple hours earlier I had indeed gotten married in Miami! Evidently I had rushed off with the keys to the rental car in my pocket. This was perhaps the first indication for my new wife Nancy, but certainly not the last, that she had married an absent-minded professor. So she was forced to rush out and catch a plane to Atlanta to see if she could catch me before I departed for Cyprus. I wasn't allowed to exit the plane to apologize to my wife, so all

I could do was to sheepishly hand over the car keys to the stewardess. The stewardess gave me a disapproving look, and took the keys to my wife, who was waiting patiently (?) outside the door of the plane.

Later that week Nancy and her mother joined me in Cyprus for the second conference, which was taking place with Evangelicals for Middle East Understanding and Middle East Council of Churches. Nancy's mother, however, was very concerned that we not disclose that we were already married, so as not to spoil the wedding to come in Bethlehem. After all, a number of people from the conference would be attending. So of course we had separate rooms.

Importantly, however, while at this conference we were able to make connections with Jonathan Kuttab, a person who was to become crucial for our paths going forward, both in terms of our upcoming wedding in Bethlehem, and regarding our "impossible idea" for an International Pilgrimage in 2000.

Jonathan Kuttab was a Christian Mennonite Palestinian lawyer for whom peacemaking is a way of life. As one of the leading human rights lawyers in Israel and Palestine, he had in the early 1980's co-founded Al-Haq, a non-governmental human rights organization in Jerusalem. He also co-founded the Palestinian Center for the Study of Non-violence, and in 1990 co-founded the Mandela Institute for Political Prisoners.

So it was that at the conclusion of our conference in Cyprus, upon arriving in Palestine, with Jonathan Kuttab's help we got permission to get married in the Lutheran Christmas Church in Bethlehem on Saturday, October 10th, 1992.

We had chosen this date for a specific reason. In the Hebrew calendar, the 10th day of the seventh month was a very special day. Every 50 years this date was to be the day when the year of Jubilee was declared—a blessed year of restoration, healing, and new beginnings! (See the Book of Leviticus, Chapter 25:9-11). In the ancient Hebrew calendar, the first month of the year began at the beginning of spring. So when calculated as best we can from our Western calendar, the 10th day of the seventh month would be October 10th, our Jubilee day of new beginnings!

Of course, sometimes things carefully planned can get complicated in unexpected ways. On the morning of our wedding I went over to the Christmas Church in Bethlehem about 11 A.M. to look over the situation. We were supposed to get married around 1 P.M., but when I got there the Church was locked. I was told that the key was with a young boy who had gone home for lunch. Meanwhile, while I was waiting outside, the day was declared a "strike day" in support of Palestinian prisoners who were being held without adequate medical attention in Israeli prisons. This meant that all shops in East Jerusalem (where Nancy was), and in Bethlehem, were to close immediately! So now the shop where Nancy had just been fitted for her wedding dress was closed. Thank goodness Jonathan Kuttab was able to convince a friend to open another shop momentarily, so that Nancy could be fitted for another wedding dress. This of course took some time.

On top of that, due to the "strike day" declaration, vehicles coming from Jerusalem were only allowed to come part way into Bethlehem. So people coming for the wedding from Jerusalem would have to walk up the hill to reach Christmas Church. I anxiously waited several hours in front of the Church, not knowing what was going on. Finally, at about 2:45 P.M. the young boy with the key showed up to open the Church, the ancient organist showed up to play the Church's ancient organ for us, and the American Pastor, on sabbatical at the Lutheran Church in Jerusalem, who was to perform the marriage service, came walking up the hill to join me in front of the Church. He soon filled me in on what had been happening. Then at 3:00 P.M. my lovely bride-to-be came struggling up the hill in high heels in her beautiful wedding dress, along with her daughter Clara. Clara had arrived several days earlier, and had somehow been able to locate some flowers that morning before shops were closed.

So finally, our wedding got under way. Joining us for our modest ceremony, in addition to Jonathan Kuttab, were several other members of the EMEU community who were at the conference in Cyprus the past week, including Dr. Don Wagner, who had many years experience working for Palestinian human rights, and Pete Hammond, the Director of Inter-Varsity Christian Fellowship's Marketplace programs. Also Michael Anderson from Chicago, staff member and illustrator for *Cornerstone Magazine*. Thankfully, Michael had a video camera and was able to record the entire ceremony (every year on our anniversary Nancy and I enjoy watching it one more time!).

Another person who was going with us on our Holy Land tour, and was able to join our humble wedding gathering, was Burnett Thompson from Washington, D.C., one of the leaders of the National Prayer Breakfast held in D.C every February, who the following year was able to get us an invitation to attend that year's National Prayer Breakfast. Finally, Bill Warnock, head of World Vision's Jerusalem office, and his Assistant, Virginia Woodward, graciously honored us with their attendance as well. Dr. Don Wagner, Clara, and Nancy's mother each read Scripture in the service.

Nancy's wedding dress

Following the wedding ceremony our Palestinian hosts took us down to the Church of the Nativity, marking the place where Jesus was born, to receive a blessing from one of the Priests. This is a traditional ritual for couples married in Bethlehem. To this day, Nancy and I always say, "married in Bethlehem, married to Bethlehem!". Later that evening Nancy and I went to the American Colony Hotel in East Jerusalem for a brief two-day personal honeymoon (finally!), while our tour group went on exploring the Holy Land without us. Later, we joined them, along with Nancy's mother and daughter Clara, for the rest of the tour.

Our first experience after we rejoined our tour group was visiting the so-called "International Christian Embassy" in West Jerusalem. After a few brief introductions, Jan Willem van der Hoven, the founder and head of the Embassy, took the floor. He began with a brief summary of the purposes of their mission—to connect Christians from around the world with Israel, and inform them of what he believed to be God's purposes for that nation. Among the Embassy's goals was encouraging the building of the Third Jewish Temple on the Temple Mount. Then he went on a long rant disparaging all Palestinians in Israel and Palestine, both Muslim and Christian. He warned those who planned to travel to Bethlehem to be extremely careful, as their lives would be at risk because of "the Arabs there with their long knives".

I was shocked to hear him carry on this way. We had just come back from Bethlehem and everyone had treated us wonderfully. But more than that, back in 1966-67 I had spent a year in Jordan and Palestine on a one-year study-abroad program with Fuller Theological Seminary in Pasadena, California. I split my time that year living in Amman, Jordan and East Jerusalem, both of which at that time were under the control of the Jordanian government. When in East Jerusalem I often visited up on the Mount of Olives with this same Jan van der Hoven and his wife, Vidad, who was an Arab Christian. He described himself at that time as "a missionary to Arabs". It was from him that I first learned to have love and concern for Arab people, and spent many hours in prayer with him for all Arab people living in Israel, Jordan and Palestine.

So what happened, I wondered? When he finally finished his rant, I raised my hand. I asked him, "Mr. van der Hoven, do you recognize me?" He said, "no". So I reminded him of the hours I spent in 1966-67 up on the Mount of Olives learning how to pray for Arab people— from him, in his living room. This completely caught him off guard. He became nearly apoplectic, spewed out some words in Hebrew, and hurried off the floor into a back room. Someone else came forward to answer any other questions. Our meeting was soon ended.

After our wonderful experience in Bethlehem just a couple days earlier, I think this experience with the so-called "International Christian Embassy"—and van der Hoven's diatribe against the Arabs in

Bethlehem, "with their long knives"—strengthened our resolve to find a way to lift up the people of Bethlehem and Palestine. I would later learn that following the "Six Day War" in June of 1967, he and his wife moved down from the Mount of Olives to the Israeli portion of Jerusalem, and he later founded the International Christian Embassy (with some suspected financial help from Israel). I also learned that his two children, born in Israel to his Arab wife, subsequently served in the Israeli army, and converted to Judaism.

At any rate, we continued our tour of the Holy Land for another week. We visited the site of the Mount of the Beatitudes (see Luke 6. 20-49) where I was able to give a talk explaining the context of Jesus' sermon. We, along with Nancy's mother and her daughter Clara, had a wonderful time.

At the conclusion of our tour, Nancy and I flew to Chicago to attend a meeting of "The Gathering", which brought together Christian foundations from around the country. In fact, it was at this same gathering of foundations several years earlier in Washington, D.C., that I first met both Nancy's mother and Nancy, when I was serving as the Executive Director of Jubilee Foundation in Chicago. Our contacts with some of these folks would later prove useful when we were seeking other people to join us in providing help for the struggling Churches and children in Bethlehem and throughout the Middle East.

Perhaps it was the stimulus of our exhilarating experiences in Bethlehem and the Holy Land that two months later, during Advent season in 1992, my new bride Nancy and I came up with our wild idea. We were preparing for a Christmas Bible Study, and read together the story of the visitation of the Magi in Chapter 2 of Mathew's Gospel.

Somehow the same idea popped into both of our heads (this happens to us a lot). The 2000th anniversary of Jesus' birth was before us in eight years. What if we tried to reenact the original Journey of the Magi for

Jesus' birthday in the year 2000? We could organize an international caravan of Christian Pilgrims, and like the original Magi, travel on foot and by camel following the same 1500 miles route from Iran to Bethlehem! We were very excited about our idea, and couldn't wait to share it with others.

Later that week we were out at our new home in the mountains of California sledding on the snow with my children. We told them about our wild idea, and they all broke out laughing. "No way!", was their unanimous response. But later, as we were walking back to the house, my son Mark said, "Dad, I know you. You are going to do this, and when you do I want you to take me with you!". That was a rare snip of encouragement that I would hang on to for the next eight years!

Over the next few months we began to share our wild idea with a few other friends and Christian leaders. The almost unanimous response was like the first response of my children: "No way!". And they all of course had many good reasons for reaching such a conclusion. No way would it be possible to get permission to do this in Iran, or in Iraq or Syria for that matter. For instance, seriously, how would anyone be able to get permission from Saddam Hussein in Iraq to allow a caravan of Christian Pilgrims to pass through his country? Nothing ever happened in Iraq without Saddam Hussein's personal stamp of approval. We would face a similar problem of having to get permission from President Hafez al-Assad in Syria. Also, just the physical and logistical challenges of leading such an international caravan of Pilgrims over 1500 miles, on foot and by camel, through five Muslim countries, to arrive in Bethlehem on Christmas Day, 2000, would seem highly unlikely, and probably, as many had already told us, impossible.

On top of those challenges, it occurred to us that there might be an even bigger obstacle. How would we ever be able to get the permission necessary to have a part of the celebrations taking place in Manger Square in Bethlehem on Christmas Day in 2000? Some had suggested that there could be as many as 5 million Christians coming to Bethlehem from all over the world to honor Jesus on His 2000th birthday. How would it even be remotely possible for our hoped for International Pilgrimage to have any role in Bethlehem on such an august occasion?

CHAPTER TWO

---✦---

FOCUSING ON BETHLEHEM—1993 TO 1996

After discussing the many serious obstacles that lay before us, we decided that the first thing we needed to do was to actually start with exploring Bethlehem. Sometimes it is wisest to explore how we might secure the end goal of our destination first—being part of Christmas Day in Manger Square in the year 2000—before investing in the groundwork for the beginning of our hoped for Pilgrimage in Iran, Iraq and Syria. If the end goal is truly impossible, then what's the point of wasting money on trying to develop the starting point?

So it was that me and my 13 year old son Mark flew off to Palestine just before Easter of 1993. Thank goodness we would now have the wise council of such community leaders as Jonathan Kuttab, and World Vision's Bill Warnock to guide us. Once we arrived in Jerusalem, we decided that the first thing we might want to do is show some respect for the indigenous Church leaders, and go talk to the Patriarchs of some of the ancient Churches that had been on the ground there for centuries.

I first managed to get an appointment with the Latin Catholic Patriarch of Jerusalem, Michel Sabaah. He was the first indigenous Arab Patriarch of the Latin Catholic Church in 500 years. He graciously granted me an interview, and I described to him our dream of reenacting the Journey of the Magi on foot and by camel for Jesus' 2000th birthday, hopefully arriving in Manger Square in Bethlehem on Christmas Day in 2000. Then I asked him for his permission and his blessing. He was very kind, and said that of course we had his blessing to undertake such a venture. "It would be wonderful to do such a thing", he said. But he wanted me to know that, honestly, from what he knew (and he knew a lot), "it would be impossible".

In the next few days I was able to arrange meetings with Diodoros I, the Patriarch of the Greek Orthodox Church, and Torkom II, the Patriarch of the Armenian Orthodox Church, and ask for their permission and blessing as well. And their response was similar to that of Patriarch Sabaah: a wonderful idea, but of course in the end, "impossible!". But they also graciously gave us their blessings, and their permission for us to try for the impossible.

Thanks to Jonathan Kuttab, on this first trip I was able to meet with Bishara Awad, the President of Bethlehem Bible College. Their work is very important here in Bethlehem, and we look forward to finding ways to be part of it. Also thanks to Jonathan Kuttab, I learned of a meeting that was going to take place in Bethlehem the following night with Christian and Muslim Palestinians, who were coming together as part of a peace-building initiative for the community. I decided I would attend and try to meet a few community leaders. But the next night there was pouring rain. I figured the meeting probably would be canceled, but I went down just to check it out, and discovered a very large crowd of enthusiastic people—Muslims and Christians—turning out in the rain to talk together. I was encouraged by their determination, and by their spirit of hope for their community. I hoped that in the future we could in some way be part of their efforts on behalf of the community in Bethlehem.

While I was attending the EMEU/MECC conference in Cyprus back in October, I had been able to make contact with Gaby Habib, the General Secretary, and one of the cofounders, of the Middle East Council of Churches, and to get his contact information in Cyprus. So I called him on the phone from our hotel in Jerusalem and was able to make an appointment to meet with him there in Cyprus in a few days. At that time there were no flights from Israel to Cyprus, but I was able to get a flight from Amman, Jordan, to the Larnaca airport in Cyprus.

When I was here in the Middle East 25 years ago, we used to be able make the trip from Jerusalem to Amman, Jordan in just over an hour. At that time Jordan was in control of everything from the Jordan River to the old walled city of Jerusalem, as well as Bethlehem. The border with Israel was on the West side of the old city. Now the situation was totally different. Since the "six day war" in 1967 Israel controls all the land down to the Jordan River. In order to cross over into Jordan, you have to go through Israeli security in front of the Allenby Bridge, and then take an Israeli bus that goes several miles out into the so-called "no man's land". Then you depart that bus and take a Jordanian bus over to the Jordanian passport office. What used to take something close to an hour, now can take up to 4 hours or more—if everything goes right.

At any rate, the next day Mark and I left Jerusalem and traveled down the hill to go over the border into the Hashemite Kingdom of Jordan. Mark and I checked through the Israeli passport office and took the two bus rides up to the Jordanian passport office. But when we got there, and tried to enter into Jordan, we were met by a surprise. In order to enter into Jordan, one needed first to apply for a visa in the Jordanian consulate's office back in Jerusalem. This was something new. No one had told me about this.

So now what? While we sat on a bench trying to get over the shock and pull ourselves together, someone I recognized came walking in. It was Joseph Donnelly, who worked for Patriarch Sabaah in Jerusalem. Since the Patriarch served the Latin Catholic churches in both Israel and Jordan, Mr. Donnelly often traveled to Jordan on the Patriarch's behalf. I figured he might have some pull with the Jordanian security guard at the passport window, so I asked him if he could help us. For a moment I was hopeful that God had sent someone to rescue us out of our dilemma. But the Patriarch's secretary had some bad news. He told me that this had once happened to him, and the only recourse was to go all the way back to Jerusalem, and go the next day to the Jordanian consulate to apply for a visa. If everything went smoothly, we would be able to be back at the Jordanian passport window that we were now sitting in front of—in maybe two days.

I slumped down on the bench. This would mean that we would not be able to get to the Amman airport in time to get our plane to Cyprus, in order to meet with the General Secretary of the Middle East Council of Churches. I had been hoping that we could ask Gaby Habib to have MECC partner with us in doing our hoped for International Pilgrimage, as this would perhaps give us some credibility in the region. Otherwise, we would just be some crazy Americans with an impossible idea that we hoped could happen—if ever—in eight years. I really didn't know what to do. I explained to Mark our situation, and asked him to pray with me for direction in how to handle our new dilemma. We sat there and prayed for more than an hour.

However, just when we were about to get up and drag our bags and my broken spirit back to Jerusalem, the man in the Jordanian passport window called us over. He asked me to tell him what we were doing. I tried to tell him as briefly as possible why we needed to get to Amman, and what the Secretary for Patriarch Sabaah had said we had to do—to go back to Jerusalem and start over. Then he asked to see our passports. The next thing I knew he was stamping our passports, and with a kind smile, told us to "move on through!" I told Mark, "the Lord heard us!" We grabbed our bags and took the next bus into Amman. The next day we were on our plane to Cyprus to keep our meeting with Gaby Habib.

In 1985 the MECC office had moved from Lebanon to Limassol, Cyrus, because the airport in Beirut was often under siege during the years of the Lebanese civil war. We landed in Larnaca, and took a taxi to their office in Limassol, where we met with Gaby Habib and his wife, Kathy. We had some traditional afternoon tea, while talking with them about our idea of reenacting the Journey of the Magi for Jesus' 2000th birthday. Gaby was somewhat skeptical of our idea. MECC had staff in Iran, Iraq and Syria, and he knew first hand some of the many problems we would no doubt encounter. But his wife Kathy was enthusiastic, and encouraged us to "go for it!" When we left them, Gaby said to stay in touch, so I remained hopeful that down the road we might be able to form some kind of co-sponsorship with MECC. This could be an enormous help for our progress in Iran, Iraq and Syria. Mark and I flew home to California feeling that we had at least made a good start on some of the challenges that lay before us.

In the summer of 1993, Nancy's daughter, Clara Pascal, reconnected with Bill Warnock and Virginia Woodward of World Vision in Jerusalem. Over the next year or two, she worked closely with them in rebuilding homes in Bethlehem for families whose homes had been demolished by various Israeli factions. During that time she took a picture of some Palestinian children behind barbed wire, and my wife Nancy made it into a poster, with the following passage from Proverbs. The poster would eventually become distributed internationally.

PROVERBS 24:11-12

Deliver those who are drawn
    toward death
And hold back those
    stumbling to the slaughter
If you say, "Surely we did not
    know this".
Does not He who weighs the
    hearts consider it? He understands
    all hearts, and he sees you.
He who guards your soul knows you knew.
    He will repay each person
        according to his deeds.

On September 13th, 1993, a very important event took place in Washington, D.C. The Oslo I Accords were signed in a public ceremony by PLO Chairman Yasser Arafat, Israeli Prime Minister Yitzhak Rabin, and U.S. President Bill Clinton. The Accords provided for the creation of the Palestinian Authority, which would assume the responsibility of managing the West Bank and Gaza with an interim self-government. They also provided for the withdrawal of the Israeli Defense Forces from Palestinian territory administered by the Palestinian Authority. The PLO acknowledged the right of Israel to exist, and pledged to reject violence, and Yasser Arafat was allowed to return to the Palestinian occupied territories as head of the Palestinian Authority.

So when Nancy and I returned together to Bethlehem in the spring of 1994, there was some hope among many of the Palestinian people that the Oslo I Accords would lead to the reduction in the number of settlers taking over Palestinian land, and help in their desire for the future establishment of a separate Palestinian State. At the time of the Camp David Peace Accords back in September of 1978, there were approximately 7500 Israeli settlers in the West Bank. By September of 1993 there were probably something over 100,000 Israeli settlers in the West Bank. Despite the Oslo Accords, however, the numbers would only continue to grow.

On this trip we met again with Bishara Awad, the President of Bethlehem Bible College. We shared with him our wild idea about our "impossible" Pilgrimage, and he was very supportive. We also connected with Naim Ateek, the Canon of the Anglican Church at St. George's Cathedral in Jerusalem, and the founder of Sabeel Theological Centre. He would later become a very influential backer of our hope to create a non-government organization (NGO) in Bethlehem, committed to strengthening communities for the future in Palestine.

In October of 1994 we learned that the United Methodist Church's Board of Directors for Volunteers in Mission announced a campaign to promote a new initiative put forth by the Middle East Council of Churches. MECC now had a new leader, the Rev. Dr. Riad Jajour, and he was asking for teams to come to the Holy Land to work with the Palestinian Christians there.

Unemployment in Palestine was at nearly 50%, and despite the Oslo Accords, the West Bank was heavily occupied by the Israeli military. Many Christians were leaving Bethlehem and Palestine. Help was needed to sustain the presence of Christians in Bethlehem, and to work with them in planning for Christmas in the year 2000. We were encouraged to see that there were others who were beginning to recognize the potential of Jesus' 2000th birthday to bring resources for strengthening Christians in the Holy Land. This also gave us more hope that we might be able to secure MECC as a co-sponsor of our International Pilgrimage at some time in the future. This gave us additional encouragement to press forward on pursuing our hope of staging an International Pilgrimage to honor Jesus on His 2000th birthday.

In 1995 we made several more trips to Palestine to better understand the needs of both Christians and Muslims in Bethlehem and Jerusalem. On one of these trips we took my three children and stayed in the American Colony Hotel, where we had gone on our honeymoon. We also traveled together to Bethlehem, and made a few more friends there.

We agreed to contribute to several important projects at Bethlehem Bible College that would strengthen their role in the community, including their program to feed families in need. My wife Nancy was an enthusiastic support of this program.

My Children on a Camel in Jerusalem

On September 28, 1995, a further interim agreement was made between Israel and Palestine with the Oslo II Accords, signed by Israel's Prime Minister Yitzhak Rabin, the Palestine Authority's Yasser Arafat, and President Bill Clinton. By this time the number of settlers in the West Bank had increased to over 150,000—not exactly the reduction in numbers that Palestinians had hoped would occur following Oslo I. And to put an even darker picture on the future of a Palestinian State, on November 4th of 1995, Yitzhak Rabin was assassinated in Tel Aviv by an Israeli person who believed that all of Palestine should belong to Israel, and objected to any sort of agreement with Palestinians.

In November of 1995, our friend Rev. Dr. Donald Wagner was appointed as the Executive Director of the Center for Middle Eastern Studies at North Park University, a Christian University in Chicago. This was the first evangelical Christian Middle East Studies Center in North America. We were able to secure a modest grant to contribute to the fund for establishing the Center, in gratitude for Dr. Wagner's important voice of encouragement urging us to continue seeking to make our dream of an International Pilgrimage to honor Jesus on His 2000th birthday a reality.

FOOTNOTE: For more about Dr. Wagner, see his book, *Dying in the Land of Promise: Palestine and Palestinian Christianity from Pentecost to 2000.* Second revised edition, 2003, by Melisende.

Finally, in the spring of 1996 we were able to take an important step toward making possible our hope of having a role in the festivities in Manger Square for Christmas of 2000. Jonathan Kuttab was able to establish for us a non-government charity in Jerusalem. After much discussion that spring about the best name for our NGO, we agreed on the name **Holy Land Trust**. Several important community leaders agreed to serve on the founding board, including Rev. Dr. Naim Ateek, and Jonathan Kuttab. Our hope was that Holy Land Trust could not only serve as the facilitator for securing our participation for Christmas Day in 2000, but would then continue in the years going forward to serve as an incubator for much needed community projects.

We returned in the fall of 1996 to Bethlehem, and were able to meet Bishara Awad's son, Sami Awad. We shared with Sami our hope of reenacting the Journey of the Magi for Jesus' 2000th birthday, which we were now calling the *Journey of the Magi 2000: A Pilgrimage for Peace.* By this time, one Christian Orthodox denomination in Jerusalem had indicated their desire to adopt our wild idea for an International Pilgrimage, but they wanted to reserve it for just their own Church people. Nancy and I, however, insisted it must include every Christian group--Protestant, Catholic, and Orthodox—and Muslims as well. Sami was very enthusiastic about our plan, and our desire to include everyone.

During our several conversations with Sami, we also learned some important information concerning Sami's background. Back during the First Intifada, which began in December of 1987, Sami's Uncle, Mubarak Awad, had played an important role in organizing non-violent demonstrations and acts of non-violent resistance. As a teenager Sami badly wanted to participate in Mubarak's demonstrations. However, as time went on violence against the demonstrators increased. In the first 13 months of the First Intifada 332 Palestinians and 12 Israeli's were killed. In light of this, Sami's family sent him away to live with family members in Kansas in the U.S. Sami eventually graduated with a BA from the University of Kansas, and pursued a Masters degree from American University in Washington, D.C., where his Uncle Mubarak Awad was heading up the ministry of Non-violence International, and teaching at American University. During Sami's time at American University, Mubarak had been personally mentoring Sami in non-violent strategies. In the spring of 1996 Sami completed his MA in conflict resolution and non-violent action, and by that fall returned to Bethlehem.

After several more conversations with Sami, we hired him to be the Executive Director of Holy Land Trust. We described to Sami some of our vision for establishing Holy Land Trust in Bethlehem to work on behalf of the entire community of Christians and Muslims in Bethlehem and all of Palestine, to prepare for a better future. However, Sami Awad's immediate challenge would be to get Holy Land Trust, now registered in Jerusalem, to be approved by the Palestinian Authority as a recognized NGO in Palestine. His other immediate challenge would be to work with the Mayor of Bethlehem and other community leaders to allow our project to be included in the emerging plans for Manger Square on Christmas Day, 2000. When we first arrived in Bethlehem in 1993, few were looking that far ahead. But soon many Christian leaders from the U.S. and around the world would begin coming to Bethlehem seeking to be part of whatever plans were being made. Sami would give us a running head start toward making the proper connections with the decision-makers in Bethlehem.

Some of my motivation for seeking to accomplish such an engine of hope for the Palestinian people was probably rooted in my own background. I was actually born Robin Catlin in Yonkers, New York in 1941. My father, Horace Wainwright Catlin, was born on Catlin Hill just west of Owego, in western New York. Many Catlin's lived on Catlin Hill, and many others lived up and down the Susquehanna River, which runs up through Pennsylvania into western New York. One of the Catlin families living along the Susquehanna about 60 miles south of Catlin Hill was the family of George Catlin, who lived in Wilkes-Barr. George Catlin's mother had been captured during a raid by a Native American tribe when she was a young girl, and she was treated very respectfully until her release. So she taught her son George to treat Native American people in the same way.

Being a self-taught artist, George wanted to record the appearance and customs of Native American peoples before their culture was forever altered by America's new settler culture. So in 1830 George Catlin traveled with Governor William Clark (of the "Lewis and Clark expedition" of 1804-1806) on a diplomatic mission from Saint Louis up the Mississippi River into Native American territory. Over the next five years George Catlin made 5 similar trips up into Native American territory and visited 50 tribes. Then he traveled 1900 miles up the Missouri River to the North Dakota-Montana border, and visited with 18 more tribes. Over 600 of his paintings and artifacts resulting from these trips eventually became part of the Smithsonian Museum in Washington, D.C. But this only happened a few years after his death in 1872. During his lifetime George Catlin was often referred to in a derogatory manner, as "that Indian lover". However, because of his remarkable paintings, by the early 1900's he was being referred to as "the great George Catlin". Too bad he never got to hear that during his remarkable life.

What George Catlin did throughout his life was to give a voice to the voiceless Native American people. He wanted to portray them as human beings, who had a culture of their own often worthy of our admiration. He once described his anguish over the reality that Native Americans were facing. When a settler on the East Coast was killed by a Native American, the newspapers would scream loudly about the "savages" who had done this. But when an entire village of women and children were slaughtered out on the plains, there was only silence. They had no voice with which to address the settler culture concerning their unjust reality. As it says in Proverbs 31:8: "Speak out for those who cannot speak, for the rights of all the destitute." So George did just that throughout his life. George Catlin tried to tell people the plain truth, saying, "One day these brothers and sisters will rise up at the Resurrection and bear witness to what we have done. And what will we say?"

FOOTNOTE: For more on George Catlin, see his **Letters and Notes on the North American Indians**, 1841, and **The Last Rambles Among the Indians**, London: Sampson Low, Son, and Marston. Marston House, Ludgate Hill, 1868.

So an important part of our motivation in seeking to do our International Pilgrimage is to help Americans become aware of the Palestinian Christian presence in Bethlehem, and the vital role they play in the entire Bethlehem community. They are deserving of our prayers, and our lifting up our voices on their behalf.

CHAPTER THREE

TRYING TO SOLVE THE OTHER "UNSOLVABLES" 1997 TO 2000

While we had no guarantees at this point, we felt confident enough in Sami Awad, and his presence on the ground in Bethlehem, that we could now give some of our attention to the other countries that would be involved in our Pilgrimage.

Another part of our motivation in creating an International Pilgrimage of Peace for the year 2000 was to shine a light on the existence of the many different Christian communities we would encounter on our 1500 miles journey—communities for which many of us in American are not even aware of their existence. In addition, in too many of our newspapers, all too often Muslims in the Middle East are portrayed as "terrorists". But we hoped on our Pilgrimage to introduce, as well, the graciousness and generous hospitality of so many within the Muslim communities we would encounter while traveling through four Muslim countries.

Despite all the increasing difficulties growing between Israel and Palestine, there were a few key people back in the U.S.A. who always encouraged us to push ahead, and try to make our wild idea happen, no matter what. One was of course Rev. Dr. Don Wagner, who was there with us for our wedding in Bethlehem in October of 1992, and has remained a constant source of encouragement ever since. Another significant person who offered us encouragement was Dr. Landrum Bolling. Nancy and I were able to connect with Dr. Bolling at the National Prayer Breakfast. Dr. Bolling, a Quaker, had served from 1958 to 1973 as the President of Earlham College in Indiana. In 1968 he accepted a special assignment from the American Friends Service Committee to examine the role Quakers could play in the search for peace in the Middle East, and published the group's finding in **Searching for Peace in the Middle East,** American Friends Service Committee, 1970.

Dr. Landrum Bolling later worked on behalf of President Jimmy Carter as a backdoor channel between the head of the Palestinian Liberation Organization, Yasar Arafat, the Israeli Prime Minister, Menachen Begin, and Egyptian President Anwar Sadat. Dr. Bolling passed notes back and forth between them and Jimmy Carter in preparations for the successful Camp David Peace Accords, which were signed on September 17, 1978. This resulted in the first signing of a peace agreement between Israel and any Arab country with the agreement between Israel and Egypt, signed on the White House lawn in March 26, 1979.

FOOTNOTE: Dr. Bolling's last book was ***Ending the Israeli-Palestinian Conflict: Arab-Jewish Partnerships****. 2014, by Piedmont Press.* Several years before his death, Dr. Bolling sent Nancy and I a Christmas card with a note suggesting "it might be time to do the Pilgrimage for Peace again!" He died on January 17, 2018, at the age of 104.

These two men, Rev. Dr. Don Wagner and Dr. Landrum Bolling, had significant positive experiences working in the context of the Middle East, so we trusted them above others. Despite all the doubts and reservations of many, with their on-going encouragement we resolved to keep trying to push forward and make our wild idea happen. We were now ready to begin exploring the situation on the ground in Iran, Iraq, and Syria.

We were starting from scratch in Iraq. In 1991-1992, following Saddam Hussein's invasion of Kuwait, the U.S. bombed extensively in southern Iraq, where in fact many Chaldean Christians lived. We also bombed extensively in northern Iraq, including in Kurdistan, where Assyrian Christians lived in the area around Mosul, having fled to there when they were driven out of Armenia and Turkey in 1913. But very few people in America, including many Christian congregations, knew that there were some Christian communities underneath these bombs in both the north and south of Iraq. How could we help make American Christian communities aware of these Christian communities in Iraq?

This is where we felt our reenactment of the Journey of the Magi might be of help. The Magi are one of the most recognized "brands'" worldwide. The visual image of "three guys riding on camels" is right up there with Coca Cola! Sometimes, one needs to use the familiar to lead people into discovering the unfamiliar. Our idea was that by reenacting the Journey of the Magi, we might be able to capture people's attention long enough to introduce them to the unfamiliar—the Christian Churches in Iraq, as well as in Iran and Syria—many of whom had been there for well over a millennium before Christianity was introduced to America.

An equally distressing aspect of America's war with Iraq back in the early 1990's were the sanctions placed on all kinds of supplies. The impact of these sanctions meant that Iraqi hospitals were not able to treat some of the simplest medical needs, and many children in Iraq were needlessly dying from the lack of even the most basic medical supplies. By 1996 it was reported that many children each year were dying for lack of food and adequate medical supplies, and many of the elderly as well.

Nancy and I both found the reality of these innocent children dying to be horrible. But what could we do? Thankfully, we discovered that an American humanitarian organization, **Conscience International**, founded by Jim Jennings, had somehow developed connections on the ground in Iraq, and was bringing medical supplies into the hospitals in Baghdad. We contacted Jim Jennings and offered to make a grant to his organization to help deliver additional medical supplies into Iraq. So it was that in the spring of 1997, with the help of Jim Jennings and **Conscience International**, I was able to make my first visit to Iraq.

Nancy and I decided that, initially, I should go alone and assess the situation on the ground. Because of the embargo against Iraq, it was not possible to fly into Baghdad. So I flew into Jordan and made arrangements to take the only available route at that time to get into Bagdad—a 10 hours trip across the desert departing from Amman, Jordan. My driver had already made one trip from Bagdad to Amman that day, so to stay awake on the return trip he put in a tape of "The Macarena". It was on a repeat mode, so every 6 minutes it would play the same song over. And over. And over. Very loudly! For the first 6 hours, I thought I would go crazy, but eventually it wore me down and melted my mind, and I started to really get into it—I found myself jiving in my seat to the beat of "The Macarena".

We drove across the desert at about 130 kilometers per hour. I stayed awake the whole time, because I couldn't possibly sleep with that loud music, and also I could see that the driver was sometimes starting to nod off on occasion, so I would give him a poke and make conversation for a few minutes. Upon arriving in Bagdad, I learned that foreigners were expected to stay at the Al Rasheed Hotel, where all the rooms were, of course, bugged. To make a phone call to America, one had to make an appointment with the desk. In about 30 minutes, one would get a call back saying the call could go through. Listening in on these calls would be someone from Iraqi security. In the first several days in Baghdad, I would call Nancy each night about 9 pm when I got back to my hotel room. But one night Jim Jennings of **Conscience International** was able to get me an appointment with General George Sada. General Sada at one time was the top ranking Christian in the Iraqi Air Force, and was the current President of the National Presbyterian Church in Baghdad, with over 1000 members. Having served formerly as an Iraqi National Security Advisor, he had many extensive contacts within the Iraqi government. He could be just what we needed to make possible our Pilgrimage through Iraq.

Thankfully, General Sada was very excited about the idea of reenacting the Journey of the Magi, and we spent several hours discussing how this might be possible in Iraq. I didn't get back to my hotel room until after midnight. I was very tired, and I decided not to call Nancy that night. However, shortly after I got back into my room I got a call from the person who "supervised" my calls each night. "Mr. Robin", he said, "you didn't call your wife?" I explained that I was tired, and had decided I would call her tomorrow. He told me, "Mr. Robin, you must call her. It's a love story!" So we did call that night as usual. Nancy of course was glad to hear from me, as she had been praying for me every night since I left. Without divulging too many details (Iraqi security was listening in to our every word after all), I told Nancy that I thought we perhaps had found the crucial contact to make doing the Journey in Iraq at least a possibility. General George Sada.

Because of his extraordinary connections, over the next couple of days, General George Sada was able to secure for me an appointment with one of the top Security officials in the Iraqi government. When I came into his office, he was very blunt and to the point. "Why are you here?", he asked. It was too soon to go into our Journey plans—we would leave the introduction of that idea to General George Sada. So I simply said, "God told us to come!" I mentioned that we disagreed with our country's sanctions on Iraq's medical supplies, and that we had come to help the children. "Good", he said, "Thank you for coming!" Then he shook my hand. That was it—the meeting was over. So far, so good!

Later that week, traveling back across the vast desert from Baghdad to Amman, Jordan, I was feeling greatly encouraged about our prospects for actually being able, against all odds, to do our International Pilgrimage. However, while I was exploring the situation in Iraq, some unfortunate developments had taken place in Palestine. Northeast of the city of Bethlehem is a hill called Jabal Abu Ghneim, which was covered with more than 60,000 pine trees and has been an ecological reserve of sorts. On top of that hill is the buried remains of an ancient Byzantine Monastery that dates back to the 5th and 6th centuries. Pilgrims of that era, after visiting the Church of the Holy Sepulcher, would pass through this Monastery on Jabal Abu Ghneim on their way to the Nativity Church in Bethlehem.

In 1991 Israel declared the entire hill to be "state land", even though most of the hill belonged to a number of Palestinian property owners. So the Palestinian owners were no longer allowed to build on their property. The site of the ancient Monastery and several other ancient Christian holy sites nearby had never been adequately explored by archaeologists. Nonetheless, in March of 1997 construction was begun there on a new Israeli settlement, and whatever remained of this Christian Monastery and the other holy sites was simply bulldozed away, along with all the pine trees. The goal of the new Jewish settlement, now called Har Homa, was to extend the encirclement of Jerusalem on the southeast with high rise buildings, which would allow for an additional 30,000 to 40,000 settlers to occupy Palestinian land. This massive new settlement would also block any possibility of the expansion of the village of Beit Sahour, lying two kilometers south of Har Homa. Over the next several years, as we all watched these high rise buildings marching steadily down the hill, the hope that was offered by the proposed terms of the Oslo Accords in 1993 was steadily eroded. This was very discouraging for many Palestinian communities, and for us as well.

By August of 1997 Sami Awad had become very much involved in the plans of the radio station Bethlehem 2000 to promote preparations for events for the year 2000. This would include promoting our **Journey of the Magi 2000: A Pilgrimage for Peace.** To this end, we were able to arrange for a small grant to help Radio Bethlehem 2000 increase its broadcast range, to include Jerusalem and Ramadi in the north and as far south as Hebron.

In the fall of 1997 we were also able to partner with World Vision in Jerusalem, now led by Tom Getman, to create a matching grant to feed some of the families and children in Bethlehem who were now suffering because of the lockdowns happening so regularly in their community. We were also able to arrange a modest grant to aid some families of the Jalahin Bedouin tribe. Originally a nomadic tribe who had inhabited the Negev for several centuries, they were removed from their tribal lands in 1952 by the Israeli military, and resettled in the open lands east of Jerusalem. They were promised at that time that this would be their new permanent home. But in 1997 a number of these families were removed from the land that had been promised to them earlier, in order to make room for another emerging Israeli settler encampment, and were moved to some metal shipping containers in East Jerusalem. No longer having access to the sheep they had been grazing for food and income, their were utterly destitute. Nancy and I were able to meet with them several times in 1997, and wanted to help them survive until they could figure out their next move.

We saw these kinds of efforts as part of our "Gifts of the Magi" project, related to our intended International Pilgrimage for Peace. The original Magi brought gold, frankincense, and myrrh—gifts appropriate for the newborn king. So what kinds of gifts would be appropriate to the Prince of Peace today? My wife Nancy felt that any gifts that might help children cope with difficult circumstances over which they had no control would please Jesus, who had said, "Whoever welcomes a little child in my name welcomes me." (The Gospel of Matthew, Chapter 18:5). As for helping the Jalahin Bedouin, I remember singing in church the words of a Christian hymn, "Lord of all, Lord of all, Jesus is Lord of all". So if Jesus is Lord of all, including the Jalahin Bedouin, at least we could try to provide for some of their families some food rations to help them out in their present crisis.

Also in the fall of 1997, MECC had moved their office from Cyprus to Beirut, Lebanon. So we were able to travel to Beirut to meet with their new General Secretary, Rev. Dr. Riad Jarjour. We had been hoping to get MECC to be a co-sponsor of our International Pilgrimage. So we shared with Dr. Riad Jarjour our plans for our Pilgrimage, which included caravanning through Syria on our way to Bethlehem. Dr. Jarjour was originally from a small Christian village in northern Syria called Al-Hafar, where his modest Presbyterian Church did its best to minister to the Christians of the community, as well as to the needs of their nearby Muslim neighbors. While at first somewhat skeptical of our "impossible idea", he said he might even consider allowing MECC to be a co-sponsor of our International Pilgrimage. Hallelujah! This could make a huge difference in giving our International Pilgrimage some credibility, and would be a wonderful answer to our prayers!

Nancy and I gave our attention to several other issues that now needed some immediate work. One was easy—with Nancy's permission I started growing a much longer beard. In the Middle East, men with white hair and long white beards are respected—and perhaps thought to be a Christian or Muslim holy man (wish being a "holy man" was that easy). This could be very important on our Pilgrimage when walking through Iran, Iraq, and Syria. By the year 2000, my beard would be as long as the Patriarchs I visited in Jerusalem in the spring of 1993!

The second issue was more complicated. Now that we had a charitable organization underway in Palestine, we needed to accomplish the same thing here in the U.S. Fortunately, my friend and colleague Phil Elkins knew Pete Holzmann, a person who was involved with the U.S. Center for World Mission in Pasadena, California. Pete had a non-profit organization named DataServe that had been approved by the State of California and the I.R.S., but at the time was no longer operating. He offered to make it available to us for free. This would save us a lot of time and money going forward. All we had to do was revise the description of our mission a little, name a new board of directors, and do a legal name change, and we would be in business! We called our new non-profit The Magi Corps. Phil Elkins would become our Director of Operations. Going forward, Phil and his wife Norma would work tirelessly to manage every aspect of The Magi Corps, in preparation for and execution of our International Pilgrimage in 2000.

Early in 1998 Nancy and I traveled together on the 10 hours trip across the desert from Amman, Jordan to Baghdad, Iraq, to meet up again with General George Sada. On this trip we traveled with General George to explore the route we would be traveling on foot and by camel in the fall of 2000. General George was able to secure an invitation for us to visit with the leadership of the Abu-Nimr tribe. Their name translates into English as "Father of Tiger"—a tribe famous for their fierce courage. Their territory included the town of Ramadi, just north of Fallujah, in the Al Anbar Provence. We were able to join the leadership of this tribe in a very large tent, along with a number of other tribal members who had gathered there to petition the Sheikh on other matters. Nancy and I felt very honored that we were being allowed to be part of such an impressive gathering.

The meeting was being chaired by Sheikh Abdul Razaq. There were also about 10 local leaders gathered there with him who were part of his leadership council. They were dressed in traditional Sunni Arab clothing, including the keffiyeh headdress and a long gown. To begin the evening, the local leaders introduced themselves to us. To our surprise, however, many of them spoke to us in very clear English. Even more surprising was the description of many of their backgrounds. One had graduated from the Harvard School of Medicine. Another was a graduate of Massachusetts Institute of Technology with a Ph.D.

in science. And so it went around the room. After graduation, each of them had come back to serve their people. Now we were more than impressed.

Eventually, we were asked to report about our plans for an International Pilgrimage on foot and by camel through Iraq. Our goal was to follow as closely as possible the original route of the Magi, who had traveled through Iraq 2000 years ago on their way to Palestine seeking "the newborn king". We would be praying a blessing of peace upon all those we passed along the way. We hoped to arrive in Bethlehem on December 25th, 2000, to honor Jesus on His 2000th birthday. We asked for their permission to pass through their territory in October of 2000. Sheikh Abdul Razaq conferred briefly with his leadership council, and then assured us that we would be very welcome to travel through their territory. He even offered to have some members of the Albu-Nimr tribe accompany us on horseback as we passed through! We were very encouraged by the positive reception we received.

Later that spring Nancy and I traveled up to Al Hafar in Syria to meet with Dr. Riad Jarjour, the head of MECC, in his home village. His village was in crisis, because their well had run dry due to an on-going drought and the subsequent large drop in the water table. All their fruit trees were close to dying, and growing other crops was becoming impossible. This also impacted their Muslim neighbors nearby. They hoped to dig a much deeper well that would save their village, along with their Muslim neighbors. Dr. Jarjour had arranged for us to meet with some of the Presbyterian and Orthodox Christian leaders of the village. They had been told that we hoped to provide some help toward getting the new well done.

The elders stood in a line, and Nancy went around and shook each of their hands. In Arab culture shaking the hands of a woman is typically not done. But they were very eager to get help with their well! They described to us their hopes for the new well, and it's importance in saving the orchards of the village. Then Nancy announced to them that her mother, Rhoda Ware, wanted to make a grant from her Foundation toward the completion of the well. Immediately the elders broke out into a chant: "Rhoda, Rhoda, Rhoda, Rhoda!" This was to be another of our "Gifts of the Magi" to honor Jesus.

We got an update in July from Sami Awad in Bethlehem about progress being made there. Up to now, Holy Land Trust has been sharing an office in Jerusalem with the Palestinian Center for the Study of Non-violence. Sami has been working with them on setting up meetings between the Palestinian Legislative Council and citizens of the community. He has also been working closely with the Christian Peacemaker Team (CPT) on protecting homes that have been threatened for demolition by the Israeli military. And he has started conversations with the Israeli Peace group Gush Shalom exploring ways that they can work together. This was very encouraging news!

In October of 1998 we were in Chicago for some planning meetings, so on the following day we traveled up to meet with Dr. Don Wagner at North Park University. Don had arranged for me to speak in a meeting with the Middle East Student Association, sponsored by the University's Center for Middle Eastern Studies. I made a presentation to the students about our planned Pilgrimage. Following my presentation one of the students approached me to learn more. His name was Peter Thiep.

He was originally from South Sudan, a member of the Catholic Christian portion of the Nuer tribe. He had grown up in the midst of war, and saw two of his best friends go off into the bush to fight against the northern part of Sudan, controlled by an oppressive Arab government. Both were killed. Peter considered joining the war, but his elders urged him to leave the village and go to the city to pursue an education. They told him, "We need some educated people who will be able to tell the world about our situation, and someday bring peace".

Thankfully, Peter was able to register as a refugee with U.S. customs, and immigrate to Sioux Falls, South Dakota, along with other Nuer refugees. Eventually, because of Dr. Don Wagner's Center for Middle Eastern Studies, he was able to register as a full-time student at North Park University.

Peter Thiep shared with me something that was important to him from Isaiah 18:1-7. Here Isaiah describes a tall people of bronze complexion (his people) for whom major disasters were occurring. In verse 7 it describes how his people went up to Jerusalem (Zion) to seek relief from "the Lord of hosts".

He saw our Pilgrimage as a vehicle by which he could take the message of his people to a global stage, and to go up to Jerusalem on behalf of his people in hopes that the current war in his country might cease. He would be graduating in the spring of 2000. He asked if there was any way he could join us on our Pilgrimage. We desired for our Pilgrimage to be an International Pilgrimage, and since Peter was from South Sudan, and spoke Arabic, he would be an important asset for us. So of course I invited him to join us following his graduation.

In the first week of November in 1998 we attended the conference held by Evangelicals for Middle East Understanding at the National Presbyterian Church in Washington, D.C. Some of our new friends were there as presenters, including Dr. Gary Burge, New Testament teacher at Wheaton College.

FOOTNOTE: See Dr. Gary Burge's recent important book, ***Whose Land? Whose Promise? What Christians are not being told about Israel and the Palestinians,*** The Pilgrim Press, 2013).

Another presenter at the conference was Brother Andrew (Andrew van der Bijh), the founder of Open Doors International. He is widely known for smuggling Bibles "behind the Iron Curtain". After the fall of Communism Brother Andrew shifted his attention to the Middle

East. As he shared with us at this conference, he was now seeking to call attention to the plight of Palestinian refugees in Lebanon, and to the needs of Arab churches in Lebanon, Israel, and Palestine.

FOOTNOTE: See his books, ***Light Force: A Stirring Account of the Church Caught in the Crossfire of the Middle East Conflicts***. Fleming H. Revel, 2004, and ***Secret Believers: What Happens When Muslims Believe in Christ***. Fleming H. Revel, 2007.)

One of Brother Andrew's favorite sayings was, ***"The Bible is full of ordinary people who went to impossible places and did wonderful things simply because they decided to obey God"***. Earlier in the year we had shared with him our hope of creating an International Pilgrimage to honor Jesus on His 2000th birthday, and Brother Andrew has since become one of our most enthusiastic supporters for doing our Pilgrimage in 2000.

At the end of November we heard from Sami Awad that they have now moved the Holy Land Trust office to Bethlehem, where they share office space with Bethlehem 2000 radio.This means that Sami will now be able to work very closely with them on preparations for Christmas in 2000. Also, Brian Davidson of Missionary Athletes International in the U.S. had met with Sami Awad in Bethlehem back in October, and we have now learned that the Charlotte Eagles soccer team has been given permission to enter Gaza and play a game in the National Stadium against the Palestinian national team on December 10th this year. This would be the very first game to ever be played in the new stadium built by the E.U. in Gaza!

The Charlotte Eagles soccer team arrived in Jordan on December 2nd, including several members of the team who would later become our future Pilgrims—Keith Dakin, Todd Elkins, and Prosper Kwenda. Over the next several days they did a radio show for the Voice of America, and shared their testimonies with several churches in Amman. And they played several soccer games in the Jordanian National Stadium before departing for Israel on December 7th. Unfortunately, Prosper Kwenda from Zimbabwe was denied entry into Israel, and unable to play in the game against the Palestinian National Team in Gaza. After touring Jerusalem for several days, the rest of the Charlotte Eagles were able to gain entry into Gaza.

I was able to join them on Thursday, December 10th, and watched them play the National Palestinian team in the new National Stadium to a 5 to 5 draw. Passing through Gaza customs on my way back to Jerusalem later that afternoon, I heard several Palestinian security guards, having received word about the game, excitedly announcing in loud voices, "We tied the Americans! We tied the Americans!"

Charlotte Eagles Soccer Team in Gaza

In January of 1999 we began working on creating logos for Holy Land Trust in Bethlehem, for our International Pilgrimage, and for the **Remembering the Innocents** festival on December 28th. The one designed for Holy Land Trust in Bethlehem incorporates an image of the Star of Bethlehem with the horizon of the earth—suggesting the Incarnation.

Holy Land Trust Logo

The second one is for our Pilgrimage itself, which we have named **Journey of the Magi 2000: A Pilgrimage for Peace**. Here again, the Star of Bethlehem is incorporated, along with an image representing praying hands, together with the horizon of the earth, indicating the purpose for our Pilgrimage—praying for peace on earth, and peace for all the people we would encounter on our 1500 miles journey to Bethlehem.

Journey of the Magi 2000: A Pilgrimage for Peace

The third logo is for Holy Land Trust's plans to celebrate "Remembering the Innocents" on December 28th of each year, following Christmas festivities. On the traditional Church calendar, this date is noted to remember the innocents killed by King Herod following the departure of the Magi. Now, the intention is to enlarge that perspective, and remember all the innocents still suffering in Bethlehem and around the world. The logo utilizes the photo taken by Nancy's daughter Clara, showing children behind barbed wire.

Remembering the Innocents

In early February we were able to legally change the name of our non-profit corporation from Magi Corps to Holy Land Trust USA. During the first week of February Sami Awad was able to join me in a meeting with Dick West and the board of Westwood Endowment, where we shared our vision for our **Journey of the Magi 2000: A Pilgrimage for Peace**. On February 11th we received word that we would receive *a* $25,000 grant from Westwood Endowment toward our International Pilgrimage. I expressed my appreciation to Dick West and his board for their ministry of encouragement to us through their gift. In this same letter, I shared a personal reflection on our struggles to date: "Sometimes it is hard for me to tell if we are leading a parade just a little out in front of others, who will be following shortly, or if we are just way out there lost in the desert somewhere. Sometimes it feels a bit scary to be out there all by ourselves. The only thing that has kept us going (and kept me from quitting) was the realization that even if it turned out that we were out there all alone, God was out there far in front of us, and was leaving signs of His presence and activity along the way to encourage us to press on, and try to catch up with Him."

On March 10th of 1999 I received a fax from David Bentley of Zwemer Institute. I had first met David and his wife Isabel when I was living in Jordan back in 1966-67 on my "year abroad" program sponsored by Fuller Theological Seminary. They had been living there in Jordan for a number of years as missionaries, and I learned a lot from them about Muslims and Arab culture at that time. David's fax included a handful of pages from his new book, *The 99 Beautiful Names of God: For All The People of the Book.* In the Qur'an, Muslims, Christians and Jews are referred to as "the People of the Book". We were subsequently able to make a grant toward having it published by the William Carey Library before the end of year. On our Journey, we planned to begin each day with prayer, meditating on one of these 99 names as described in David's book.

In March of 1999 we receive another piece of good news. Holy Land Trust in Bethlehem has now been approved by the Palestinian Authority as a legal NGO in Palestine. Sami Awad is now working with several community organizations in planning for Christmas in December of 1999. This will help further strengthen Holy Land Trust's desire to play a significant role in plans for Christmas in 2000 in Bethlehem, and create a space for **Journey of the Magi 2000: A Pilgrimage for Peace** to have a part. This news was so encouraging to us. Sami has done more for us in Bethlehem than we initially thought would be possible. We thank the Lord for Sami Awad, and his team at Holy Land Trust.

In mid-March Nancy and I flew into Amman, Jordan, and traveled by car up to Damascus, Syria. We had received word from Dr. Jajour that MECC would join us as co-sponsors of the **Journey of the Magi 2000: A Pilgrimage for Peace**! Our prayers were being answered! We met with Dr. Jarjour and the Syrian country coordinator for MECC, Mahat el-Khoury, who apparently has connections with everyone in the government. Through the urging of Dr. Riad Jarjour, she had arranged for us to meet with several of the cabinet members for President Assad, including the Deputy Minister of Tourism and the Director of Tourist Relations. We explained to them our hope for an International Pilgrimage to travel through Syria on foot and by camel on our way to Bethlehem for Jesus' 2000th birthday. They had many questions for us, and doubted that we could actually do this, but in the end they said, "On behalf of President Assad, you have permission to travel through Syria". This means that another one of our "unsolvable" problems has been solved! We are very grateful to Riad Jarjour for his role in bringing this about.

In the following week, Nancy and I traveled with Jim Jennings of Conscience International to visit once again with General George Sada in Baghdad. But this time, rather than traveling the 10 hours across the desert from Amman to Baghdad, we were now able to go down through Syria into Iraq. There were some good reasons why we had not been able to go into Iraq by this route before. The border between Iraq above Al Qa'im up to Abu Kamal in Syria had been "sealed" for many years with land mines for miles on both sides of the border. While preparing to follow in the footsteps of the original Magi, I read a number of books seeking to discern the actual route taken by them. One of these books, published in 1995 by Paul William Roberts, describes Roberts being led through this maze of landmines by a Bedouin guide. Unfortunately, Roberts' camel got her leg blown off by a land mine—luckily for Roberts it wasn't his leg! So here was one more very big "unsolvable" concerning our desire to follow the original route of the Magi.

However, we learned that some time in the previous year something astonishing had happened. The land mines had all been removed so that trucks could move contraband oil from Iraq through Syrian into Turkey! Another one of our "unsolvables" had been solved! After first hearing about this, for the first time since beginning our quest seven years ago, some of my own doubts were removed about attempting our "impossible" Pilgrimage. Maybe the Lord really did want us to do this!

At any rate, we departed from Palmyra on that spring morning and ran into a fierce sand storm. It was blinding and we couldn't see anything. The intrepid Jim Jennings wanted to push on ahead, but our Bedouin guide from Palmyra strongly suggested we turn back. So turn back we did. By late afternoon things had cleared up enough to set out again, but as we got down near the border above Abu Kamal we decided it might be best to spend the night in a very modest truck stop before crossing the border. Very modest would be a modest way to describe it. It was filthy. I do not think a woman had ever darkened the door there until my brave Nancy entered. Nancy and I got a room that had one narrow little cot with a unique mattress. It was filled with seashells. Yes, seashells! At one time a million or so years ago this desert had been a seabed. So it was smart to use seashells as mattress filling to avoid letting any bad things such as bugs or mold infect the mattress. However, I can testify that the seashells were a little lumpy. So I had my Nancy sleep on top of me all night to avoid the lumps. That was also somewhat lumpy I suppose. But Nancy is a very brave person.

General George Sada had been able to secure visas for us all to enter Iraq through this northern border station. So the next morning we arrived at the Iraqi border security, only to find them being very perplexed as to how we managed to get our visas. We actually had to sit there for more than 8 hours while they tried to contact Baghdad to see if our visas were legitimate. Finally, they got word back from someone in Baghdad that we were okay, and they let us pass on through. Once we were across the border into Al Qa'im we found a store that had some soccer balls, and we bought all that they had so we could share them with young men playing soccer that we passed along the way. Nancy also bought a lot of candy for the children we might see in villages we passed through on our way to Baghdad. To this day, more than 20 years later, Nancy can still picture the young boy who received a candy bar from her running like the wind to go hide under a bridge to make sure that no one took it away from him.

During our time with George Sada in Baghdad, we decided it would be good to go 15 miles south to visit Ctesiphon. At the time that the Magi would have been traveling on their way to Jerusalem, Ctesiphon was serving as the ancient winter capital of the Parthian Empire—when the snows made their summer capital at Ecbatana impassable. So the Magi would have passed through here. Therefore, when traveling out of Iran in October of 2000 to follow the original route of the Magi, we would make a stop here. By the 5th century Ctesiphon had become a very large city, but all that remains above ground today is the grand arch covering the former palace. Built of brick, the vault is 120 ft. high and over 80 ft. wide. It is considered to be the widest single span vault of unreinforced brickwork in the world. Impressive. But it was not yet there when the Magi passed through. It was built several centuries later.

Thanks to George Sada, we were also able to meet that week with the head of the Iraqi Ministry of Antiquities. He was quite interested in our planned International Pilgrimage, and after some discussion he pledged to create the costumes needed by our four Magi to represent what would have been worn during the Parthian period in question. The following day George took us out to visit Kohe, the site of what may be the oldest dedicated church building in the world, dating back to perhaps 70 A.D. Later that week we met with several people in charge of the management of Kohe, and encouraged them to consider giving the ancient churches that responsibility in light of it's historical significance for Christianity. We will have to see if this outcome happens. Meanwhile, we have a lot of thanks to give to George Sada for all that he has been able to accomplish for us thus far. And also to Jim Jennings of Conscience International, as well, for introducing us to George.

In June we were in contact with Dwight Gibson, North American Director of World Evangelical Alliance. I had worked closely with him on another project a few years back when I was Executive Director of Jubilee Foundation. We learned that he was traveling to the Philippines soon, and we filled him in on our plans for an International Pilgrimage. While in the Philippines he met with Augustin Vencer, the General Secretary of the World Evangelical Alliance, and told him about our plans. His son John Vencer was there in the Philippines at the time, and also heard about our plans. John immediately volunteered to join us on our journey. This was great news! He would be a great addition to our International team of Pilgrims!

In late July we had some important meetings in San Diego with several consulting firms to help us develop plans for marketing our International Pilgrimage. We met again in late September, but by the end of the year we had to terminate our relationships with all of them. They all were coming forth with huge budgets to accomplish the grand plans they were proposing. Wonderful plans—but we realized that we could not afford to move forward with any of their plans. They were very disappointed in us. And we were disappointed and discouraged as well—we had not been able to get as many individuals and foundations to join us in our dream as we had hoped for. After considering all that was involved, many potential funders came to the same conclusion that so many others had come to from the beginning—a wonderful idea, but in the end, impossible.

For several years now we had been having discussions with people here in the U.S. and in the Middle East about what our attire should be on our Pilgrimage. Some in the U.S. warned us that whatever we do, do NOT to wear white like Pilgrims do when traveling to Mecca.

They thought that Muslims would take offense. However, Muslims throughout the Middle East had the opposite response: you MUST wear white, otherwise people would not understand that you were on a Pilgrimage. So we have now settled that discussion. We will wear white on our International Pilgrimage!

At the beginning of October of 1999 Sami Awad came from Bethlehem and met us in Washington, D.C. to attend another conference on the Middle East. Following the conference, we met with several members of Congress. The most successful meeting was with Representative Tony P. Hall, representing the district of Dayton, Ohio. A few years later he would be nominated three times for the Nobel Peace Prize. At the moment, thank the Lord, Tony Hall became quite interested in what we were attempting to do to honor Jesus for the year 2000. He listened carefully and took notes as we and Sami explained the purpose of the **Journey of the Magi 2000: A Pilgrimage for Peace,** and our hope that our International Pilgrimage could help lift up and encourage the Christians in Bethlehem, and the rest of Palestine and Israel, and hopefully throughout the Middle East as well. After some of our recent discouragement, we were greatly encouraged by Congressman Tony Hall's interest in our Pilgrimage.

Soon we would be even more encouraged, and actually, greatly astonished! As a result of our meeting with Congressman Tony Hall, on Thursday, November 18th, a formal recognition of our **Journey of the Magi 2000** was entered into the Congressional Record by Congressman Hall as follows:

Congressional Record

United States of America

PROCEEDINGS AND DEBATES OF THE *106th* CONGRESS, FIRST SESSION

WASHINGTON, FRIDAY, NOVEMBER 19, 1999

THE JOURNEY OF THE MAGI

HON. TONY P. HALL
OF OHIO
IN THE HOUSE OF REPRESENTATIVES
Thursday, November 18, 1999

Mr. HALL of Ohio. Mr. Speaker, as we approach the new millennium, our focus has been, more or less, with Y2K issues rather than the fact that, for Christians around the world, it represents the 2000th anniversary of the birth of Jesus.

To those and many others, the new millennium provides a rare opportunity for new beginnings and renewed hope which will challenge all people of goodwill to rededicate themselves to the principles of justice, mercy, forgiveness and peace—precepts made more fundamental by the conflict, turmoil and suffering sadly evident in the lands of the Bible and throughout the world.

In this spirit, church families of the Middle East, both ancient and modern, are inviting peace-loving people to join them in celebrating this opportunity and this anniversary commemoration. Sponsored by the Holy Land Trust, part of the commemoration will be a historic reenactment of the Journey of the Magi, the original pilgrimage of the three wise men over 1,000 miles to Bethlehem to witness and honor the birth of Jesus.

This historic undertaking will have pilgrims from many nations traveling for 99 days by foot, horse and camel along ancient caravan routes through six countries that make up the holy lands of the Bible, commencing in mid-September of next year and ending on December 25th in Bethlehem.

Like the three wise men who brought offerings of peace to Bethlehem, the participants in the Journey of the Magi 2000 will also bear modern day offerings. During each day of the 99 days of the trip, humanitarian assistance will be given to the needy people of the country through which the travelers pass.

This pilgrimage of peace is being coordinated by the Holy Land Trust and the Middle East Council of Churches, as an expression of the deep-seated desire of church families of the Middle East to seek peace and peacemakers. We appreciate the spirit and purpose of this event, as well as the incredible challenge it represents, and believe it deserves our support.

We trust that all people of goodwill will encourage and support the Journey of the Magi 2000 and other efforts to relieve suffering and promote peace as a fitting entry into the new millennium.

Here is part of the declaration made on the floor of Congress:

WHEREAS, through international television broadcasts, educational programs and an interactive web site, these modern day pilgrims will share their hopes and activities for peace with the world, and **enable all people of good will to follow in the footsteps of the Magi**, and participate with them in seeking peace and the renewal of hope as a fitting tribute to the 2000th anniversary of the birth of Jesus;

Now, therefore be it

RESOLVED BY THE HOUSE OF REPRESENTATIVES (the Senate concurring),

That it is the sense of **Congress** that the **United States of America** should be among the first nations of the world to support the spirit and goals of this historic **Pilgrimage for Peace**, and, further, the United States government and all other governments representing people of good will, in the lands of the Bible and around the world, should likewise encourage and support **The Year 2000 Journey of the Magi** and all related efforts to relieve suffering and promote peace as a fitting entry into the new millennium.

I think this was a turning point for Nancy and I—after so many people telling us that our "wild idea" was in fact, impossible—now we had a resounding affirmation of our hope for an International Pilgrimage from nothing less than the United States Congress! Who would have thought this could happen?

Sami also had some great news for us from Bethlehem. He had received word from Mrs. Arafat's office (the wife of Chairmen Arafat) accepting her role in the **Remembering the Innocents** celebration planned for December 28th, 1999. Incredible! Things were beginning to come together.

Meanwhile, we had been working with Phil Elkins for several months on securing visas for a trip to Iran. We still needed to secure permission to caravan through Iran in September of 2000. We also wanted to investigate our route from Hamadan (the former ancient city of Ecbatana) down to Iran's border with Iraq. We were trying to squeeze the trip in before the snows came to the mountain areas around Hamadan. On Nov. 3rd our visas were confirmed for me, my son Mark, and Todd Elkins. The Rev. Dr. Riad Jarjour of the Middle

East Council of Churches sent us some contact information for the Evangelical Synod of Iran and the Assyrian Evangelical Church, as well as for several other Church bodies in Iran. We hoped to receive their guidance on what acts of mercy would be most appropriate for the people of Iran. Phil Elkins sent them letters informing them of our upcoming visit, and of our hoped for Pilgrimage in Iran in September of 2000. Unfortunately, the only response we got back was a telegram from one Church body indicating that it would be "unsafe" for them to meet with any Americans. Very sad.

Our plan was to depart from the L.A. airport on the evening of November 11th, and fly to London Heathrow airport, where we would then fly on to Tehran, Iran. Mark and I flew into the L.A. airport that day and met up with Todd. Norma Elkins had gone into L.A. to pick up our documents, but got stuck in traffic working her way out to the L.A. airport. When the line began to form for boarding our flight to London Heathrow, Todd and I got in line to save a place for us, and we sent Mark out to the curb to meet Norma. At the last minute Norma arrived at the curb, and Mark grabbed our passports and rushed in just in time for us to board the plane.

Arriving in Tehran on Nov. 12th, we were welcomed by our tour agent Sam Sadeghi. The next day he took us to meet with some Iranian officials. This was my 58th birthday, but no birthday cake for me today. However, everyone was very cordial, and a brief tour of Tehran had been arranged for us, including visiting a magnificent Cathedral. We didn't expect to see such a Church here in Iran.

The Saint Sarkis Cathedral of the Armenian Orthodox Church

By November 15th we arrived in Hamadan. My son Mark and Todd Elkins played some soccer with some local youth, while we worked on finding a local climbing guide.

Mark Playing Soccer with Youth In Hamadan

48

On the 16th we traveled out with our local guide to climb the 11,729 foot Mount Al-Avand. In September of 2000 our plan was to climb this mountain (sacred in the history of Iran) and spend three days in prayer and fasting near the summit, before descending back down to Hamadan to depart on our International **Pilgrimage for Peace**. The trail up to the summit of Al-Avand is steep. There were several huts established at intervals up the mountain where families could rest and share a picnic before continuing on up the mountain, or going back down. While it was common at this time to see the portrayal of Iranians on American television as mobs of people shouting "death to America", the families gathered there on the mountain—many with their children—were very excited to meet Americans. They graciously offered us sandwiches and fruit and cookies. It was their hope that Iran could soon renew a positive relationship with America, and resume the tourism that had once been an important pillar of their economy.

Eventually, Todd, Mark and I reached the summit, carefully negotiating the last 30 feet of the sheer rock face of a pinnacle at the very top. We wished we could have stayed longer. However, we gave whatever food we had left to a few hikers who had managed to reach the summit, and headed back down to Hamadan. The next day we departed Hamadan and drove down from the hills through Kangavar to the major city of Kermanshah. Spending the night in a hotel there, we continued on down to the border city of Qasr-e-Shirin. All along the way we identified places we could camp when traveling by foot and by camel during September of 2000. Returning back through Hamadan to Tehran, we felt that we had learned enough on this trip and made sufficient arrangements to make our Pilgrimage through Iran the following September very doable. And we had received approval from Iranian officials to travel through Iran. We now had Iran and Syria secured as venues for our International Pilgrimage. One more to go—Iraq!

So in the spring of 2000 Nancy and I made one more 10 hours trip across the desert from Amman, Jordan to Baghdad, Iraq to meet up with General George Sada. We spent several days with General George Sada going though details about the necessary preparations for our Pilgrimage in the fall. Then the next day I told George there was one more stretch of highway I wanted to drive over that we had not yet investigated. So George drove me east on the highway leading to the border with Iran. We were turned back by border security well before the border, but at least I had a good idea of the terrain we would be traveling over as we departed Iran on our way to Ctesiphon.

The following day in Baghdad General George took me to an important meeting with the head official of Iraqi Ministry of Security. We had been trying for several years to find someone able to be in touch with Saddam Hussein about our desire for permission to lead our International Pilgrimage by foot and camel through Iraq. None of the highest level Security people could give us permission for such a venture without securing the personal approval from Saddam. As it turns out, for a number of years Saddam Hussein had been sequestered in one or another of his many estates, and even his top security people weren't always sure of his exact location. He would have food delivered to a handful of his estates, so no one could tell where he was just by where food was being delivered—this at a time when many Iraqi people were going hungry and even dying from lack of food because of the U.N. sanctions.

At any rate, the head of Iraqi Security told us that he had finally been able to be personally in touch with Saddam Hussein. He was now pleased to inform us that Saddam had given his personal approval for our Pilgrimage in Iraq! Not only that, but Saddam volunteered to send 200 soldiers with us across Iraq for our protection! George and I were ecstatic to hear the news that our Pilgrimage could go forward with Saddam's personal approval! But Saddam's offer of sending 200 soldiers along with us created an awkward moment. Our Pilgrimage was to be a **Pilgrimage for Peace.** Being accompanied by 200 soldiers did not send that kind of message. How do you tell Saddam Hussein "no thanks for the soldiers", after he has given his personal approval for our Pilgrimage to travel on foot and camel through his country? Taking a deep breath, I politely informed the head of Iraqi Security to please thank Saddam Hussein for his gracious offer of soldiers, but that wouldn't be necessary. Placing my hand on the cross I was wearing, I informed him that **The Prince of Peace** would be our security. He looked somewhat surprised, but accepted our answer.

As Nancy and I returned back across the long stretch of desert from Baghdad to Amman, Jordan, we rejoiced in the knowledge that the last of the remaining "unsolvables" for our Pilgrimage—Saddam's personal approval—had been solved. Despite all the many nay-sayers, our wild idea of an International Pilgrimage was now looking actually possible! When we got back home we let our Pilgrim volunteers know that our International Pilgrimage, the **Journey of the Magi 2000: A Pilgrimage for Peace**, was **on**, and we would be departing in September as planned.

So here is our final roster of the brave souls who will make up our team of International Pilgrims, and will be traveling with us for the entire journey:

Keith Dakin, England—soccer, Charlotte Eagles
Jason Drake, U.S.—photography, satellite phone, website
Todd Elkins, U.S.—soccer, Charlotte Eagles, photography, and one of the Magi
Phil Elkins, U.S.—Holy Land Trust, USA
Prosper Kwenda, Zimbabwe—soccer, Charlotte Eagles, and one of the Magi
Andre Martinez, U.S.—video and tech
Jake Martinez, U.S.—video, tech, website
Tim McClelland, U.S.—soccer, friend of Jake
Peter Ryan, U.S.—tech, writer of content for website

Peter Thiep, South Sudan—North Park University/Chicago, and one of the Magi)

John Vencer, Philippines/World Evangelical Alliance, and one of the Magi)

Robin Catlin Wainwright—Holy Land Trust USA

Nancy Ruth Wainwright—Holy Land Trust USA

And here is our support team for the Holy Land Trust USA. office in Pasadena, California:

Phil Elkins, Director of Operations

Norma Elkins, Office Manage

George Halley, Tech (computers, satellite phones, website

There are so many others from all five countries that have also played an important role in helping us set up our International Pilgrimage—and we will forever be grateful to all of them. From the beginning, our intension has been to honor the 2000th anniversary of the birthday of the "Prince of Peace" by following the Apostle Paul's injunction in Romans 14:19: "Let us then pursue what makes for peace and for mutual encouragement". Now Lord, make it happen!

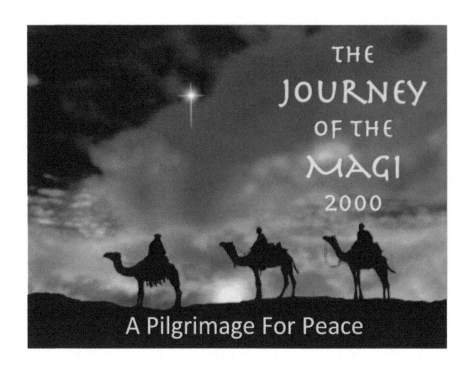

THE
JOURNEY
OF THE
MAGI
2000

A Pilgrimage For Peace

Part Two

JOURNEY OF THE MAGI 2000: A PILGRIMAGE FOR PEACE

CHAPTER ONE

◆ —— ✦ —— ◆

STUMBLING OUT OF THE STARTING GATE

We loved our plan. Todd Elkins and I planned to depart for Tehran, Iran, on September 10th, and the rest of our Pilgrim crew would arrive a few days later. In addition, there would be four additional Charlotte Eagle players who would join us for this Iran portion of our journey, as several soccer games were planned to take place as we traveled from the village of Hamadan to the border with Iraq. David Bentley, the author of *The 99 Beautiful Names of God: For All the People of the Book,* would also be joining us for the Iran portion of our journey. We would begin each day with prayer and reflection on one of the "99 beautiful names of God". Muslims rehearse these names by going through a string of 33 prayer beads three times. Almost all these names are found in our Bible, and are known to Christians and Jews, as well as Muslims.

We would all arrive in Hamadan, Iran on September 15th. Hamadan now stands on the ancient site once known as Ecbatana, the capital of the Medes and Persians, and which later served as the summer capital of the Parthian rulers. The original Magi, serving those Parthian rulers, would have departed from Ecbatana on their journey to Bethlehem to honor the newborn king, who's birth had been announced by the star rising in their eastern sky. From Ecbatana they would have traveled several hundred miles west to the Parthian winter capital, Ctesiphon, on the eastern bank of the Tigris River (in modern day Iraq, about 15 miles below today's Baghdad). Departing Ctesiphon, they would travel another 1200 miles, following ancient caravan trails north along the Euphrates River in Iraq, west across vast deserts in Syria, and over the mountains of Gilead in Jordan, at 3000 feet above sea level. From there they would descend down into the Jordan valley and arrive at the Dead Sea, at 1000 feet below sea level. Crossing the Jordan River, they would then travel up the steep mountain terrain to Jerusalem to meet with Herod, expecting to congratulate him on what they thought was the birth of his son. After conferring with biblical scholars, Herod would point them to Bethlehem. Departing Herod, they would travel south 5 miles to Bethlehem to search for the newborn king. Our plan was to follow the same 1500 miles route traveled by the original Magi, and arrive in Bethlehem for Christmas Day on Jesus's 2000th birthday.

On Saturday, September 16th, we planned to climb up 11,729 foot Mount Alvand in the Zagros Mountain Range. In preparation for our **Pilgrimage for Peace**, we would spend the next three days in a prayer vigil near the summit. September 17th would be Day One, the first of the 99 names of God: AR-ARAHMAN, "God the Sustainer". The Lord had indeed sustained us through 8 challenging years of planning and preparation, filled with a great deal of doubt and uncertainty as to whether it would ever be possible to undertake such a journey, given the modern political realities within the region. And there had been many difficulties and doubters along the way. So we intended to begin our Pilgrimage by honoring the One who had sustained us through every doubt and every obstacle.

Our third day on the mountain was to be September 19th, the **International Day of Peace**, which in the year 2000 fell on the third Tuesday of September each year (in 2001, the United Nations passed a resolution establishing the **International Day of Peace** to fall on September 21st of every year, coordinating the day with the birthday of Mahatma Gandhi). Descending the mountain on the following day, we would get everything ready and depart on our Pilgrimage on September 21st, traveling in the 5th name of the 99 Beautiful Names of God: AS-SALAM, "The Peaceful One", to honor the One called, "Prince of Peace" (see Isaiah 9:6). If everything worked out according to our plans, we would arrive in Bethlehem on Christmas Eve, 2000, celebrating the 99th name of God: AS-SABUR, "God of Patient Endurance". With God's help, we would have indeed demonstrated not only our own patient endurance, but also the patient endurance required on God's part to lift us over so many hurdles and enable us to complete our journey. Beautiful plan, don't you think?

Regrettably, on September 6th we were contacted by our Iranian coordinator, Sam Sadeghi. He informed us that all our visas had been denied! What? Why? Turns out that back in late August a group identified by Iran as a Kurdish rebel group, which was living on the eastern border of Iraq, had invaded Iranian territory and traveled up the very stretch of road that we intended to be traveling down as we prepared to depart Iran in early October. After waiting to see how the situation might develop, an Iranian official on September 7th contacted us directly, and apologized for finding it necessary to cancel our visas. He expressed that they were as disappointed as we no doubt were, because they believed that our Pilgrimage would have helped put a different light on how people—especially Americans—viewed Iran. However, they could not risk having any Americans hurt, captured, or God forbid, killed while on our Pilgrimage. He urged us to come the following spring for Easter, which was very gracious on their part. However, this was not particularly helpful in our present circumstances, with our eyes fixed on arriving on Christmas Day 2000 in Manger Square.

So right out of the starting gate, despite all our careful planning, the first 300 miles leg of our Pilgrimage was lopped off. This kind of unpredictable disruption (or as many had already suggested, "predictable disruption") was the very reason that many people had given when declining to sponsor our Pilgrimage, or join us on our journey. Welcome to life in the Middle East!

Now we were hoping to regroup with our entire team in Iraq in early October. Several of us, including me, Nancy, Peter Ryan, and Keith Dakin went ahead to Palestine in mid-September to coordinate with Sami Awad and the Holy Land Trust office in Bethlehem. Everything in Bethlehem seemed calm enough at the moment, although for several days we heard sonic booms from Israeli jets overhead, loud enough in some cases to set off car alarms in the street. We of course were startled each time this occurred, although children walking about on the streets seemed to accept it as "normal".

Tuesday, September 19th, the International Day of Peace. Holy Land Trust arranged for Nancy to be interviewed on Bethlehem 2000 Radio. She explained that one of the main objectives of attempting to reenact the original journey of the Magi on Jesus' 2000th birthday was to call attention to the Palestinian Christian community in Bethlehem. Nancy concluded her interview with another important point, saying, "Unfortunately, many Christians in the West are not aware of their existence, or of the numerous other Christian communities in Iraq, Syria, and Jordan that we will encounter as we make our way to Bethlehem. Our journey will be an opportunity to introduce these other brothers and sisters of the Christian faith to those who follow our Pilgrimage from our website". Our Palestinian Christian friends at Holy Land Trust all said Nancy did great! I agree!

On Thursday, September 21st, we all departed for Jordan, along with Sami Awad. The following day we held a meeting in the Amman West Hotel with most of the team leaders from each country involved in our pilgrimage. This included George Sada coordinating Iraq, Daoud Kuttab (Jonathan Kuttab's brother) coordinating Jordan, and Sami Awad coordinating Bethlehem. We discussed how to coordinate media strategies as our Pilgrimage progressed from country to country.

Several other difficulties emerged, such as the problem of securing visas in several Arab countries for our International Pilgrims, Prosper Kwenda of Zimbabwe, Peter Thiep of South Sudan, and John Vencer of the Philippines. All three of these men were important people to get out here with us, as they were some of the international faces of our Pilgrimage team. All three of them would be dressed in the costumes of the Magi that the Iraqi Ministry of Antiquities had created for us. Phil Elkins, along with our tech support person George Halley, remained home at the Holy Land Trust USA office in Pasadena to work on these and other problems.

Saturday, September 23rd. Sami and I found three 5 feet tall walking sticks, and took them into a nearby shop to fashion them into crosses for us. The Muslim owner was very interested concerning our plan to follow the route of the original Magi from Iraq to Bethlehem in order to honor Jesus on His 2000th birthday. He said he was honored to have a small part in it, and he prayed that we would have good success.

The next day Todd Elkins and the rest of our media crew (including Jake and Andre Martinez, Jason Drake, and Tim McClelland) arrived in the Amman airport at 3 AM. They left Los Angeles on Friday and flew 10 hours to London, then had a 9 hours layover before flying on to Amman—a 25 hours trip all together! But they had no problem with visas, and all 13 bags of their media equipment passed through Jordanian customs without a hitch. Finally, almost all of our Pilgrimage team was together for the first time.

Monday, September 25th. We were able to have devotions together with most of our Pilgrims (a few were finally catching up on some sleep). We reflected on the meaning of the 9th name of God from our book: AL-JABBAR, "The Mighty One". We concluded in prayer, recognizing that we were placing our plans, and our lives, in the hands of AL-JABBAR, "The Mighty One".

Later that evening in our hotel, I talked with our team of Pilgrims about the many possible challenges facing us. We were all beginning to take a full measure of why so many had described our intended Pilgrimage as an impossible undertaking. In light of the cancellation of the Iran portion of our Pilgrimage before we had even gotten under way, I suppose it was a legitimate question as to whether any of the rest of it would be happening at all, as well.

Tuesday, September 26th. Prosper Kwenda from Zimbabwe arrived here in Jordan to join the rest of our Pilgrim crew. He will be one of our four Magi, and an important member of our International team of Pilgrims. He is also an important member of our soccer team.

Wednesday, September 27th. John Vencer, also one of our four Magi, arrived from California today. It took him some extra time to recover from the hepatitis he came down with after eating some food from a street vender in the Philippines as he was departing for the U.S. back in June. Also Peter Thiep arrived from the U.S. It has turned out that, being from South Sudan, Peter is not eligible to enter Iraq, and will have to wait here in Jordan for us until we (God willing) enter into Syria. Then he will come meet us there.

Later in the day, everyone went out to get passport photos in order to apply for their Syrian visas. Keith Dakin had to get a second passport, because some Arab countries would not let you in if you had an Israeli stamp on your passport. Unfortunately, by the end of the day we received word that our Iraq visas were delayed for a few more days.

Thursday, September 28th. At 10 AM there was an important press conference covering our Pilgrimage, with over 50 photographers, reporters and journalists. The conference started with a prayer from Archbishop Mar Thoma of Iraq's Eastern Orthodox Church. Then George Sada, Sami Awad, and I explained the purposes of The Journey of the Magi 2000: A Pilgrimage for Peace to the gathering. Earlier, our team had begun that day with reflections on the 12th of the 99 names of God--AL-BARI, the "Creator of All People". Building on the substance of our reflection that morning, I spoke with Iraq's Archbishop Mar Thoma in mind. Peter Ryan, writing in his journal, quoted my comments to the gathering as follows: "We believe that God grieves when innocent children die without reason. We, as Christians, cannot wait for political solutions. We must act now. With the help of **Conscience International**, we have been shipping in medicines and sending in doctors to Iraq to help the children. Our hope is that our Pilgrimage will be a means of expressing God's love for all people, beginning with the people of Iraq."

The large number of reporters and other media in attendance must have been a significant encouragement to our team of Pilgrims. But the euphoria did not last long. No sooner had we announced to the reporters our plan to depart shortly for Iraq to begin our Pilgrimage, than another event took place in Jerusalem that would change everything. Back in July 11th to the 25th of 2000, the Camp David summit with President Bill Cl**inton**, Israeli PM Ehud Barak, and Palestinian leader Yasser Arafat had been going on. But in the end, it failed to reach an agreement, and each side blamed the other for the collapse of the peace talks. Since the collapse of the peace talks tensions had been steadily increasing between Palestinian and Israeli factions. But on this very day, Thursday, September 28th, a tipping point had been reached.

Ariel Sharon, the Israeli opposition leader, led a large Likud party delegation on an incursion onto the Temple Mount, surrounded by over 200 Israeli riot police. The Temple Mount was the most holy site for Jews, but the Al-Aqsa mosque on the Temple Mount was also considered one of the most holy sites in Islam. Sharon's incursion onto the Temple Mount was seen by Palestinians as a gross violation of the peace process agreed to in Oslo Accords 2 back in 1995. Protests broke out, with youth throwing stones as police began firing into the Palestinian protesters with rubber bullets. The following day was

Friday, the day for prayer services in the Mosques, and following these services large riots broke out in many places throughout Israel and the West Bank. Israeli police switched to live ammunition and by the end of the day, 7 Palestinians had been killed and over 300 Palestinians wounded. It was the start of the **Second Intifada!**

This, of course, did change everything. The question of when we would actually be able to depart on our Pilgrimage was now totally up in the air. The impact of these events in Jerusalem quickly spread throughout the Middle East. We were told that our visas for Iraq were now on hold for what could be as long as a month! There was also now talk that, in light of the troubles, our recently secured visas for Syria could also be in doubt. And due to the troubles in Jerusalem, the country of Jordan now feared that protests could break out there as well. So police cars were assigned to our hotel to watch out for our security! Having the first leg of our journey in Iran being canceled was bad enough. But now we were seriously in danger of having our entire Pilgrimage canceled before we could even get started.

Sunday, October 1st. George Sada stopped by our hotel to have breakfast with our team of Pilgrims. He told us he was going to go back to Iraq today, and hoped to convince Iraqi government officials to please issue our visas as soon as possible, before all of our carefully made plans completely fall apart. We all gathered around George in a circle, and placed our hands on him, and prayed for his safety and his success. The 15th of the 99 names of God for that day was AL-QAHHAR, "The One Who Overcomes". However, things were beginning to look pretty bleak. Was it going to be all over before it even started? We could only hope that the Lord, "The One Who Overcomes", who had opened so many impossible doors for us already, had a plan for this one.

Tuesday, October 3rd. Nancy and I stayed in Jordan in order to be there when George Sada came back from Iraq with some word about our Iraqi visas. Keith, Todd and Prosper elected to stay with us in Jordan, so they could organize some soccer events with the youth. However, despite all the trouble now going on in Palestine, Andre and Jake Martinez, Jason Drake, Tim McClelland and several others elected to go back to Bethlehem. While everything seemed to be on hold concerning our Iraqi visas, they wanted to use the time to do some more filming there. So I gave the okay. Looking back, this was probably not one of my best decisions!

On their way over from Jordan to Israel, the media team saw two ambulances transferring a wounded Palestinian man from one ambulance to another, in order to take him to a hospital in Amman. Maybe this should have been the flashing red light telling them to "turn back!" But they went ahead anyway. Still, everything went fine through the first Israeli checkpoint east of Jerusalem, until they arrived at the Israeli checkpoint into Bethlehem. Then the Palestinian taxi driver was told he couldn't go into Bethlehem because his taxi had Israeli tags, and protesters might through rocks their way.

They were finally beginning to see the seriousness of the situation, and getting ready to turn back when a phantom car appeared from the Palestinian side of the checkpoint with his headlights off. He offered to take them into town. So four of them piled into the car, along with some of their gear. The driver said he would come back for the other 3 and the rest of the gear. They drove into Bethlehem, still with their headlights off. The lights were off all over Bethlehem, and the driver didn't want to attract any attention. Nonetheless, their car was soon flagged down by flashlight waving Palestinian soldiers. They were turning back all tourists into Bethlehem to avoid problems. But the driver told the soldiers that the three white guys in the back seat were Palestinian soldiers—and they waved them right on through! Awni, a staff member from the Holy Land Trust office, met them with another car, and the driver went back to gather the rest of the team and equipment at the Palestinian side of the last checkpoint.

Sami Awad called and told them that there was no way to get to Bethlehem Bible College tonight—there was chaos and fighting a block away from BBC. The phantom driver brought the rest of the team and equipment, and followed the HLT staff member to Sami's apartment. Given the circumstances, Sami's landlord allowed the team members to crash in an empty apartment. Sami came over and brought some of the usual late night Palestinian hospitality—tea and cookies! They sat together in the living room, grateful to have gotten through the checkpoints successfully, drinking tea and watching the tracer bullets flying back and forth outside the window in the valley below.

Wednesday, October 4th. Our meditation for those of us still remaining in Jordan was on the 18th name of the 99 beautiful names of God: AL-FATTAH, "The One Who Opens Doors". With violence rising throughout Palestine, including Bethlehem, it was now an open question, not only as to whether we would be able to depart for Iraq to get under way on our Pilgrimage, but whether we would be able to enter Bethlehem in December, should we ever be able to make it that far. All we can do is pray to God, "The One Who Opens Doors", to open the way for us. Despite all our many years of careful planning, there is so much that is far beyond our control.

Our media crew in Bethlehem tried to redeem the time by taking video of places that they would pass through later in December, on their way up to Bethlehem (God willing). However, before getting very far down the road, they were turned back by Palestinian soldiers, so they returned to Bethlehem Bible College. That night at 7 PM the power was cut throughout the city, and they could hear shooting begin again in the street outside the College. They sat together in the lounge area with a group of tourists from Great Britain, away from the doors and windows. A candle beneath the coffee table was the only light in the room. Outside they could hear the rapid fire of Israeli high caliber weapons, and the occasional pop pop pop of Palestinian small caliber rifles. They all huddled together and spent the next several hours in prayer, asking the Lord for the sparing of human life on both sides of the conflict.

Thursday, October 5th. This morning our media crew walked up the street toward the Israeli checkpoint, where the fighting had taken place the night before. The street was strewn with the clutter of rocks and rubber bullets and broken glass. The large beautiful Ritz Carlton Hotel that was located near the border wall was empty. Upon returning to BBC, they learned that it was now recommended that all tourists leave the country immediately. With the increasing violence, there was concern that Bethlehem might be locked down, leaving everyone unable to get out. So our media team right away made the trek once again to return back to Jordan.

Meanwhile, back in Jordan, Nancy and I got word that day from George Sada that he had somehow managed to secure visas for the entire team (Alhumdiallah—praise be to God!), with the exception of our Magi Peter Thiep. We were able to have everyone back together again for a very late celebratory dinner that evening, when our media crew dragged in from Palestine. By this time there had been over 47 Palestinians killed, and 1885 wounded, and 70 Israeli police injured by youth throwing stones.

Friday, October 6th. Today was announced as a Day of Rage in Palestine following morning prayers in the Mosques. And there were massive demonstrations in Amman that passed directly beneath our Holy Land Trust office there. Prosper, Keith and Todd traveled up to Gilead to oversee the building of a soccer field, one of a number of soccer fields that Holy Land Trust USA was preparing along our planned route through Iraq, Syria and Jordan. We see these soccer fields as more "gifts of the Magi" to honor Jesus.

Sunday, October 8th. My friend David Johnston has been able to join us. He speaks fluent Arabic, having served as a missionary in Algeria for nine years. He also taught classes at Bethlehem Bible College from 1993 to 19996. Nancy and I met David there in the fall of 1996 when we hired Sami Awad to run Holy Land Trust in Bethlehem. David was presently working on a Ph.D. at Fuller Theological Seminary's School of Intercultural Studies, but was now able to come join our Pilgrimage for several weeks. So we were very grateful to have a fluent Arabic speaker on the team as we prepared to journey through Iraq.

The media and tech crew along with our soccer players made the 10 hours drive from Amman, Jordan, to Baghdad, Iraq, arriving at the Sagman Hotel late that night.

Pilgrim Crew Departing for Iraq

Nancy and I stay behind in Jordan for several days to coordinate media strategy with Daoud Kuttab at the Amman Holy Land Trust office. Tuesday, October 10th, would be our 8th wedding anniversary, and we wanted to celebrate the occasion with Daoud and Jonathan Kuttab, and a few other Jordanian friends.

In Iraq, our soccer players played indoor soccer at the Iraqi Air Force Athletic Club for the next couple days. On most days, the sound of distant explosions from the bombs of U.S. jets could be heard from many miles further north. Despite the bombing, a quote from Jason Drake's journal stands out for me about this time of conflict and stress: "I am amazed at how kind and gracious the Iraqis are to us Americans, even as we continue to bomb their country daily".

Thursday, October 12th. Jason Drake, Jake Martinez, and Keith Dakin meet with the Iraqi Ministry of Antiquities to be fitted for some of the costumes to be worn on the Journey. All our costumes were made for us by the Iraqi Department of Antiquity to resemble what would have been appropriate for those serving Parthian royalty at the time of the birth of Christ.

Jake Martinez, Jason Drake and Keith Dakin
At the Iraqi Ministry of Antiquities

Nancy and I arrive at the Sagman Hotel from Jordan, where George Sada and his support crew of Albert, Edward, and Solomon are able to join our entourage of Pilgrims that night for an amazing dinner, with a choice of three kinds of meat (lamb, chicken, and steak), and numerous side dishes. This was true for all the remaining days we stayed **in** the Sagman Hotel.

Several of the team mentioned that the waiters seemed a little thin, and they badly wanted to share some of their food with them, which was more than they could eat, but found that this was not allowed. This at a time when the American sanctions on Iraq had by this time caused 6000 percent inflation. At one time an Iraqi dinar was worth more than 3 U.S. dollars. Now a U.S. dollar could buy more than 2000 Iraqi dinars. For this reason, the average Iraqi could not typically afford meat on a daily basis, if at all. I heard later, nonetheless, that some of our Pilgrims did manage to spirit some food away from the table on occasion, and share it with a few of those waiting on us, so they could take some of it home to their families.

Friday, October 13th. Churches in the Arab world often hold services on Friday, the same day as Prayer services at the Mosques. So today we all attend Baghdad's Evangelical Presbyterian Church. It has a large congregation of over 1000 people, and a large van ministry that brings in children from all over to participate in the Youth program. Albert attempted to translate the sermon into English for us.

Following the sermon, the three Magi (Todd, Prosper, and John Vencer) all visit the Sunday School service dressed in full "Journey of the Magi" historical garb. Our Magi enter with a slow procession down the aisle, being closely watched by a roomful of wide-eyed and giggling youth. A children's choir sing "star of wonder, star of light, star of Royal beauty bright" to us in English! Nancy is very impressed.

Saturday, October 14th. George Sada took me along on his ongoing meetings with various Iraqi officials. We of course had wanted to get our Pilgrimage under way as soon as possible. However, they were reluctant to let us get out on the open road because of the Second

Intifada going on in Palestine. Some Iraqis, knowing that there were Americans among the Pilgrims, might throw rocks at us or attempt to harm us in some way.

Today George and I also spoke at the Armenian Presbyterian Church in Bagdad, and shared our vision for an International Pilgrimage of Peace.

General George Sada and Robin Speaking
At the Armenian Presbyterian Church in Baghdad

There was a great deal of daily television coverage of the violence going on in Jerusalem and Bethlehem, and throughout Palestine. And the Iraqi government was declaring that millions of volunteers were signing up to "go throw Israel into the sea". Several weeks ago the number of volunteers had been announced as 2 million, then a week later it was 4 million, and by now it was 6 million, and growing daily. Never mind that there was no way on earth that Syria was going to allow a stampede of millions of Iraqi's to march through their country on the way to Israel. Not happening!

Sunday, October 15th. Me, Nancy, and George Sada meet with the Iraqi Ministry of Interior, pleading with them for permission to get our Pilgrimage underway. Our team of Pilgrims are all beginning to wonder if our hoped for Pilgrimage would be canceled, and we would all be sent back to Jordan.

George Sada, Robin and Nancy Wainwright
Meeting with the Ministry of Interior

Later that day Nancy joined our Soccer players, who were playing an indoor game against the Iraqi Air Force soccer team.

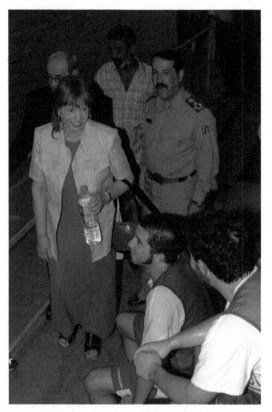

Nancy with our Soccer Players

Monday, October 16th. Today our meditation was on the 30th name of the 99 beautiful names of God. AL-LATIF, "The Kind One". That afternoon George Sada's daughter, Eve Omesh, took Nancy to visit an orphanage on the outskirts of Baghdad that was run by Catholic nuns, who were part of Mother Teresa's religious order. The orphans all represented part of the casualties of the war in Iraq. They had lost their parents in the war, but they also suffered permanent damage to their bodies. The bunker-busting bombs used throughout Iraq since 1991 had their outer shells hardened by depleted uranium, which resulted in numerous random birth defects among newborns. Most of the children in the orphanage had part of their limbs missing, or other physical deformities.

There were about 12 children in the orphanage, and most of them quite young. Nancy went around and hugged all the children one by one. The final boy she picked up had part of him arms missing—he was perhaps 2 or 3 years old. As Nancy held him up to her face, the child said to her, "momma? This just broke Nancy's heart. The nuns, seeing Nancy's tears, quickly assured her that she could just take the boy out of the orphanage with her, and that "no one would care". Of course, this was not possible for us, since we were hoping to soon depart on our Pilgrimage of over 1200 miles through four Middle East countries. But nonetheless, Nancy very much wished that she could just do as the nun's had suggested.

Tuesday, October 17th. We begin the day with a meditation on the 31st name of the 99 Beautiful Names---AL KHABIR, "The Watchful One". Then that evening, the whole group went with George Sada out to the Al-Amiriya bomb shelter. When America's war with Iraq broke out in 1991, over 300 women and children were guided into the top floor of this bomb shelter. Unfortunately, the American military knew that in fact an Iraqi military command center was operating a floor beneath the civilians crowded in to the floor above. American satellites had seen the stream of civilians entering the shelter. But this was war. On February 13, 1991 the shelter was hit with several "bunker buster" bombs able to drill through 10 feet of concrete. Cutting off electricity, the rockets made escape through the electrically controlled doors impossible. Six minutes later the next missile was a fire rocket, incinerating whoever and whatever was inside. "The Watchful One" had seen everything.

The Al-Amiriya bomb shelter had been revamped to serve as a memorial for the over 300 innocents who had lost their lives on that day. The shelter's walls were filled with framed pictures of the victims—mostly mothers and children. Various memorials were on the walls, including framed news clippings and a crayon rainbow drawing highlighting a child's simple request: "Peace for Iraq". Our plan was to hold a worship service, and then spend the next 12 hours down there in the dark on a prayer vigil, which was to be lead by David Johnston. Several hundred members from Baghdad's Evangelical Presbyterian Church had graciously come out to support our worship service. The church choir sang a few Arabic hymns for us, and then several people came up to the microphones to offer prayers, including me, and David Johnston.

I said a few words, with George Sada translating for me:

"As Pilgrims we are traveling to Bethlehem to honor Jesus on His 2000th birthday. But we cannot go on our journey, until we first come here. For the people of Iraq, this is a terrible place of pain, and suffering and death. And it is only a symbol of what was happening all over Iraq, and what has happened since for the last 9 years. God sees all things, hears all things, and knows all things. So God saw, and heard, and knows all this. We are going to stay down here and perform an all night candle-lit vigil, and offer up ceaseless prayers throughout the night. It will be dark, because this is a place of great darkness."

Robin Leading in Prayer

Then David Johnston closed our brief service with a prayer in Arabic, which David later translated for us, and below is some portions of his prayer given on our behalf: "Heavenly Father, our hearts are full of sorrow and horror in this place where so many innocent souls were martyred. Have mercy on us! Lead our hearts to a genuine repentance. O Lord our God, O Prince of Peace, bring about peace between our people and Iraq, this kindred and beloved nation! Lift this oppressive embargo from it! Grant all the people of Iraq the anointing of your Holy Spirit, and send your blessing to every part of this great country! Amen."

Robin Meeting with Family
After Prayer Service

After the worship service the members of the Church congregation soon left, and several of the Church members took Nancy back to the Sagman Hotel. Then I went down into the shelter to join the rest of the team. The lights were switched off, leaving us at the mercy of a few dozen candles. The silence in the room became overwhelming. After a group prayer the team split up into our own separate corners for silent devotions, reflecting on the lives lost, and the lives shattered by the loss of their loved ones. Imagine being one of the fathers who had stayed outside to work, but lost his entire family after sending them to the one place that was thought to be safe.

At midnight we met again as a group, reading passages from the Psalms, singing hymns, and offering prayers—pleas for forgiveness, and guidance, and strength. Most of us eventually slept some before rising at 6:30 AM for another set of devotions. Sunlight crept in from the rupture the explosion had left in the ceiling, where birds cheerfully greeted our new morning.

Thursday, October 19th. When our team first checked into the Sagman Hotel, everyone was allowed to make calls out from the hotel, and to receive calls into the hotel. After a few days here, we were allowed to make calls out, but could no longer receive calls from the outside. Now we could no longer make calls out or receive calls in. Despite the Hotel's great hospitality, it was beginning to feel like we were prisoners here. Nonetheless, our media crew somehow managed to sneak out and climb up on the roof in the middle of the night, where they could use the satellite phones to send out info to our website, and connect with some of our support team in Jordan. Don't know how they managed to do this, since there was a military camp behind the hotel, with military vehicles and people coming and going throughout the night.

Later that day, several members of our Pilgrim crew tried out their costumes that were made for us by the Iraqi ministry of Antiquities.

Costumes Made By Iraqi Ministry of Antiquities

Friday, October 20th. Today George and I are finally able to get a commitment from Iraqi Security that we would be allowed to depart with our caravan "for a few days", but then they wanted us to leave Iraq. They wanted Nancy to leave now, as they were concerned about a woman being along should there be any trouble. So tomorrow we would have to send Nancy back to Jordan. I was very unhappy about this turn of events. Given all she had been through with me to get us to this day, she deserved to be with us for every mile of the journey.

Sunset on the Tigris River

76

CHAPTER TWO

CARAVANING THROUGH IRAQ

S unday, October 22nd. Our morning devotion began with the 36th of the 99 names of God: AL-ALI, "God the Most High". I thought of Psalm 113, which declares in verses 4, "The Lord is high above all nations, and his glory above the heavens." And yet, as the Psalmist declares in verses 7 and 8, "He raises the poor from the dust, and lifts the needy from the ash heap, to make them sit with princes, with the princes of his people." So we on this day begin with the Psalmist's conclusion in verse 9, "Praise the Lord!" We are all just ordinary people. None of us has any fame or political status. And yet God has lifted us up, over, and through every obstacle, and is allowing us to honor Jesus in this way.

Today at long last is the first day of our long dreamed of and hoped for Pilgrimage to honor the 2000th anniversary of the birth of the Prince of Peace. We have lost 35 days from the time our Journey was supposed to start in Iran. But today, after so many setbacks, and so many days of uncertainty, we begin our Pilgrimage for real. But we need to keep moving. Just 65 days until Christmas!

Departing from Ctesiphon, the Western Winter capital of the Parthian Empire, situated on the eastern banks of the Tigris River, we travel south on foot and camel, until we reach a floating bridge made up of a series of pontoon rafts that cross from the eastern bank to the western bank of the Tigris. Most of the bridges along the Tigris River that connected Baghdad with Western Iraq, including this one, had been destroyed by our American military's bombing campaign in 1991. Throughout the day our caravan of Pilgrims, including 6 camels, is closely followed by hordes of excited children along the side of the road. Crossing the pontoon bridge with our entire caravan, including the camels, we reach the western bank of the Tigris River.

Todd Elkins Departing at Dawn

Crossing the Tigris River

Our camel handlers are four young men—Khalid, Oday, Sagben, and Sagmon—who are Shite Muslims from the Muslim holy city of Najaf. They will spend the night here with the camels. The rest of us turn back by car to Ctesiphon, where our media crew films our three Magi dressed in their costumes in front of a campfire under the Arch of Ctesiphon, the longest standing brick arch in the world. Actually, the Arch was not there when the original Magi passed through here on their way to Bethlehem.

Most of our support crew are Assyrian Christians, some of them cousins of George Sada. For the first handful of days our plan is to have our Pilgrim crew return to the Sagman Hotel. Each day I would return to the marker we left the previous day to resume walking. I was determined to walk every foot of the 1200 miles journey, if possible, as my personal Pilgrim's vow to honor the Prince of Peace. God willing! The camels and their handlers would stay near the spot we concluded our travel for the day, to let the camels rest up. Camels on average could manage about 20 to 25 miles a day.

Monday, October 23rd. We returned to yesterday's finishing spot on the western bank of the Tigris, and traveled north to Kohe, the site of what may be the oldest dedicated Church building in the world, dating to approximately 70 A.D. One legend has suggested that it was founded by St. Thomas, one of the 12 Apostles, or by one of disciples of St. Thomas.

Interestingly, the Parthian Empire allowed for religious diversity, so a Christian Church was allowed at this early period. However, in the Roman Empire, no dedicated Church buildings were allowed until St. Helena, the mother of the Roman Emperor Constantine, traveled in 325 A.D. to Jerusalem and Bethlehem, and began the construction of dedicated Christian Church buildings there.

On this day, a large crowd made up of several thousand members of various Eastern churches had gathered in order to commemorate Kohe, and its history. To our surprise, they had also gathered to celebrate our Pilgrimage to honor Jesus on His 2000th birthday. Our three Magi, dressed up in their costumes, rode in on their camels, and immediately a portion of the crowd gathered to welcome us. A youth choir sang some hymns for us nearby, as people crowded around us to have their picture taken. I spoke briefly to the crowd, with George Sada translating for me the following:

"We are Pilgrims from Asia, Africa, Europe and North America seeking to reenact the original journey of the three Wise Men to honor Jesus, and we have gathered here in these Bible Lands today to show the world that Christ made His Church alive here in the first century, and that by His power and grace they are still alive today!"

Departing From Kohe

Departing from Kohe, we walked another 24 kilometers by nightfall. Even four or five hours later, tour buses returning from the gathering honked their horns, and the passengers waved frantically at us, shouting "ahlan wa sahlan" (welcome!), or "marhaba" (hello!). One bus even pulled to the side of the road so that people could get out and have their picture taken with us. As Peter Ryan would remark in his journal that evening, "Never in our entire lives have any of us come this close to having 'celebrity' status. The warmth which the people here have shown us continues to overwhelm us!"

That evening the caravan crew returned to the Sagman Hotel, but George Sada and I returned to several Iraqi Security offices in Baghdad to talk further with Iraqi officials. We wanted to inform them of the great welcome we were receiving, and to ask permission to continue our way through Iraq beyond the 4 or 5 days they had granted to us. We figured it might take another 20 days to reach the Syrian border.

Tuesday, October 24th. Today we discovered that camels have a mind of their own. Very early in the day a horse and cart began following along a stretch of asphalt paralleling our dirt road. A bell hung around the horse's neck, loudly announcing its presence with a constant **clang.** As the horse and cart passed us by, Todd's camel went berserk, leaping into the air and flipping both Todd and saddle to the ground. Laughing off the fall, Todd quickly dusted himself off and, without a moment's hesitation, hopped back on the camel. Later, Tim McClelland, having already endured a barrage of green camel spit, was riding a camel that suddenly wanted to scratch an itch on her backside. She dropped to the ground, at which point Tim leapt off, and then she proceeded to roll over, as if to squash the giant human "bug" that had been riding her. Tim was fine.

Other than these two incidents with the camels, the rest of the day was flawless. On our way to the ruins of Sippar, on the eastern shore of the Euphrates, several men lay down a beautifully woven orange, black, white and red carpet at the entrance to their home. This was a symbolic gesture inviting us into their homes for tea, or whatever else we might need. We thanked the men profusely, and took pictures with all of us together, but reluctantly declined staying longer, knowing that the road ahead of us was long and that we were short on time.

As we approach the Euphrates River, we are awed by the endless fields of corn and wheat. Also by the locals continuing to invite us into their homes. It was at that moment, as we travel through one of the quietest and most peaceful areas of our journey thus far, when without warning, a rumbling could be heard in the distance—loud booms from the Southern Iraq "no-fly" zone declared by the American military, maybe fifty or so miles away. Another round of bombing courtesy of the U.S. military, that happens so frequently here that U.S. newspapers seldom bother with it anymore. There were seven blasts all together, each followed by a minute or two of silence. I wonder what the children think about this?

Reaching the ruins of Sippar, they are at first glance unimpressive. Upon closer inspection, the ground under our feet is littered with shards of pottery marked with various patterns, as well as the intact portions of heads and bases of ancient relics, shattered into pieces, but beautiful nonetheless. Sippar was an ancient Sumerian city of around the 1790's B.C. The Code of the Hammurabi Stele was probably erected here, and a cuneiform tablet containing the Epic of Gilgamesh was probably found here as well. Many of the clay tablets found here are now in the British museum.

Toward the end of the day we meet with Karagholy, the head Shiekh of a Bedouin tribe that lives nomadically between the areas of Mosa and the holy Shite city of Karbala. He brought us into their tent, which was roofed with 15 large strips woven of goat fur. Several ropes were attached to the tent and staked to the ground, from which clothes had been hung to dry. A chicken and a dozen or so baby chicks ran past us as we entered, along with a goat and several sheep. The men all sat with us, while the women peaked out from behind the tent flaps. We were served an extremely dark, and richly sweet tea served in shot glasses.

With the help of George and Solomon, I explain our intentions to caravan to Bethlehem, hoping to arrive on Christmas Day to honor the 2000th anniversary of Jesus' birth. They offered encouragement that our mission would be successful. As Jason mentioned in his journal that evening, "words can't do their hospitality justice!"

Wednesday, October 25th. We began the day with a meditation on the 39th beautiful name of God, AL-MUQIT, "The Nourisher". This theme definitely described the rest of the day for us. The people we meet on the road seem to know us—George Sada thinks we may have been mentioned in an Iraqi T.V. news segment in relation to the Kohe gathering two days ago. Today we had at least three invitations to join families for tea or lunch. David Johnston and I did take up the first invitation, but we let most of the caravan keep moving up the road.

Further up the road, the rest of our caravan met a man and his family, who were literally jumping up and down with excitement. They went in with them for tea and waited for David and I to catch up. Meanwhile, the family baked some fresh bread and provided the group with yogurt and dates. When David and I arrived, of course we couldn't just pop in, so we also shared some of the freshly baked bread along with our tea. David Johnston explained that in Arab culture, "if we are invited in and have a meal with someone, we all become like family!", and we were treated like that. We stayed for a bit longer, and then as we were leaving, we prayed a blessing upon the entire family and their house.

Thursday, October 26th. This morning, as we gathered for prayer, I called over a small child from the crowd observing us, and had him join us in our circle. His name was Yasir, and he seemed especially interested in whatever it was we were up to. I included him in our prayers, and offered prayers for the people gathered around us. Each morning following our morning scripture reading and prayer, I conclude with the exaltation to "walk and pray!", and our Pilgrim caravan hits the road. But this particular morning Peter Ryan and I remained behind to attend to our blisters. For both of us, the bottoms of our feet were covered with large blisters. We took time to let some of the fluid out, and then bandaged them pretty heavily to make walking more tolerable. Most of the crowd that had gathered around to observe our morning prayers, stayed around to see the spectacle of our feet "surgery", including little Yasir. Everyone on the caravan knew of my goal to walk every foot of the journey, but given the condition of my feet, there were beginning to be more than a few doubters!

We have now been walking for almost a week through what is famously known as the "fertile crescent" in Iraq, which stretches for nearly 200 miles between the Tigris and Euphrates rivers. As we walk along, we see women and children carrying stacks of hay on their backs three times their size. We pass a woman reaping wheat with a sickle, and later a barefoot man walking across his field with a shovel slung over his shoulder. In front of us a group of Egrets are wading through a swampy marsh. And all around us we see groves of palm trees, and irrigation canals, with endless fields of green.

Palm Trees of the Fertile Crescent

Sheep Grazing on the Fertile Crescent

Peter and I finally catch up with the rest of the caravan near the Euphrates, where they have stopped to rest up and take a break. The media crew was shooting some footage for a (hoped for) documentary on our Journey, with the "Magi" dressed up in their costumes, and riding their camels beside an irrigation canal. We all relax in the shade of a cluster of Palm trees, where a small crowd of children had gathered around Jason. One of the children begins making duck "quacks", and Jason is quick to respond with some Donald Duck "quacks" of his own, eliciting a frenzy of giggles and more duck "quacks". Jason looked over to several of us and said, "see, there is no language barrier!"

Toward the end of the day we came upon a group of young men playing soccer with a flat ball. Our soccer crew gave them one of ours, and after kicking the ball around with them for awhile, the local men showed their appreciation for the new soccer ball by gathering together, and clasping their hands on each other's shoulders in a circle, treating us to a traditional Arabic dance. One of them twirled a set of red prayer beads in the air like a cowboy's lasso, and several of them accompanied the dance with a Zimmara, a small double headed flute that sounded slightly reminiscent of bagpipes, and an impromptu drum using a bright red one gallon gas drum. A fantastic way to end another 30 kilometers day of walking.

George Sada and I continue our routine of returning at the end of each day all the way back to Baghdad to sit down with some Iraqi security officials to plead for permission to continue our journey through Iraq. We provide glowing reports of our treatment by all the people we have encountered on our way, and each day we are given permission to continue one more day. Today, being a day of prayer in an Islamic culture, is a day off, and my feet are very gratefully.

Saturday, October 28th. We began our day with a meditation on the 42nd name of the 99 beautiful names of God—AL-KARIM, God the Multiplier. And today our days of allowed travel are multiplied, and we are given permission to continue our caravan as far as Heet, which gives us almost another week! All we would need would be another week or so after that to reach the border with Syria—our hopes are rising that we may actually be able to get there.

Sunday, October 29th. The following is a quote from the daily diary of our photographer, Jason Drake. It expresses better than I can much of what is significant about our Pilgrimage.

Jason Drake: "I'm walking point again...cars fly by on bald tires a few feet to my left. I haven't seen a single tire with tread on it since coming to Iraq—tires are on the U.N. embargo list; imagine not being able to buy a new tire for ten years. From time to time a horn blares and quickly fades: back home that means, 'get off the road you idiot!' I've come to realize that in the Middle East the meaning is more akin to, 'please excuse me as I squeeze past'.

But I pay no attention to any of this. Until a white blur pulls off the side of the road directly in front of me. Then I stop in my tracks and look up thinking that perhaps I should not have gotten so far ahead. Any concern is quickly allayed, however, as the occupants of the car pile out. A couple of young children huddle together, staring, pointing, and giggling—the driver is in his early 30's and a wide smile and a sparkle in his eyes tells me right away that that he means nothing but good. Then an old woman struggles out of the car and hobbles directly toward me as if she is going to give me a horrible tongue-lashing, telling me exactly what she thinks about me and my country in no uncertain terms. But instead, both of her vein-lined, swollen-knuckled hands grab my hand and press the back of it to her lips, to her forehead, to her lips again. Four or five times she kisses the back of my hand, mumbling something in Arabic.

I'm stunned, unutterably stunned. How is it that this old Matriarch is giving me such honor? What on earth have I done to deserve this kind of accolade? How does one respond? Even if I could speak Arabic, what could I say to something like this? So I stand there, dumbstruck, uncomfortable, unaccustomed to this sort of respect. At some point I gently exact my hand from her grasp, nodding and smiling, something inadequate and banal falling from my lips. I am thankful she doesn't understand English. I slowly begin to shuffle my feet forward again, waving foolishly to the old woman. The driver of the car still stands on the opposite side of the car, but as I walk by he waves, his smile still ear to ear. He pats his chest, declaring 'Inma Christi! Inma Christi! I'm a Christian! I wave back, smiling as widely as he, and call back, 'Zen! Zen! Good! Good! For the millionth time I wish I could communicate more deeply with these wonderful people.

As I continue on through the day, the pieces of this episode fall into place. The old woman, her son and grandchildren were all Christians. They had heard of our Journey of the Magi, heard of our goals in Iraq to show solidarity with the people, to pray for them, to do what we could to aid them. And this family came out to honor and thank us for our support. And I wonder if they realize that the support they showed to me was infinitely more than anything I could ever do for them."

We continue to be greeted by people inviting us in for morning or afternoon tea. The hospitality of the people is remarkable.

Keith and Prosper Being Served Tea

Later that afternoon we are passing through the city of Fallujah, about 69 km west of Baghdad. This time, I am walking point, and there were crowds standing on the right side of the road to witness our caravan with camels and walkers passing through their city. An elderly woman, probably a widow, and all dressed in black, was standing on a raised mound just ahead. She had her right arm lifted up, and was chanting something over and over in a loud voice. Actually, I was perhaps a little alarmed (was she cursing us?), and I turned to David Johnston walking beside me, and asked him what she was saying. He told me, "She is saying, 'God bless the womb who bore you!'" Over and over. We had come to Iraq to pray a blessing upon them, and here was an elderly Muslim woman praying a blessing upon us!

Still later that day, David and I were walking toward the rear of our caravan when a very nice Mercedes pulled up and what appeared to be an older Sunni Muslim fundamentalist, with a beanie on his head, and a long white beard and robe—the kind of image that westerners are taught to fear—jumped out. He ran straight up to me, kissed me on both checks and threw his arms around me. Later, David would translate the words he spoke to me: "God's peace be upon you. God's blessing go with you. May God see you safely to Bethlehem!"

Toward the evening we were moving out of the city of Fallujah onto the open highway, leaving behind the greenery of the Fertile Crescent for the open desert. We finally stopped as we approached Ramadi, and I marked the spot with some rocks to keep track of our progress (I guess I was overly serious about wanting to walk "every foot" of the journey). Then George Sada's crew picked us all up in a bus and drove us to a restaurant in Ramadi. As our dinner orders were being taken, George and I noticed that one could order either a "half-man" or "full-man" of lamb kabobs. George and I both pounded our chests and declared, "full-man"! Well, we soon discovered that perhaps we had spoken too soon. Our meal arrived with enough kabobs to feed at least four men! Thankfully, we had some hungry walkers who welcomed the extra helpings of kabobs (nearly 20 years later, when George Sada and I get together, we still make jokes about this).

Monday, October 30th. Today David Johnston and our Palestinian cameraman Joseph had to make the 10 hours drive back across the great desert expanse to Amman, Jordan. David needed to return to work on his Ph.D. dissertation at Fuller Theological Seminary. We will miss his important role as our in-house translator.

In the afternoon I am walking out front of our caravan again when I notice movement on the horizon off to my right. Gradually I am able to recognize a young boy—maybe eight or nine—walking patiently across what could be a half-mile of desert while trying not to spill the contents of the glass he is carrying. In Islamic tradition, the one who helps a Pilgrim in some manner (water, food, lodging) will receive a blessing. This young boy's parents obviously sent the boy out across the desert to present me with a glass of water, thereby expecting for him to receive a blessing.

But here was my dilemma. Where did this water come from? If I drink it, I could get sick and be derailed from my journey with severe diarrhea (or worse). But now the young boy is standing in front of me and proudly holding up to me what is left of the water in the glass. If I dump the glass of water on the ground—which may in fact be the wisest course—then the boy will be hugely disappointed. So I offer up a prayer on my behalf that the Lord will protect me from whatever might be in this glass that could harm me, and drink it down in one gulp. Then I offer up a prayer on behalf of the brave young boy that our Lord will indeed bless him and his family for their desire to be faithful. Really wish I still had David Johnston with me to express to the boy how proud I am of him and his parents. All I can manage is a few halting words of blessings in Arabic, and the boy breaks out in a big grin and is gone.

Toward the end of the day, a farmer met me on the road with an outstretched hand. In halting English, he said, "Here, please give this money to a Palestinian family. They need it more than we do!" For us, the money he gives me is nothing, really. But for a farmer trying to raise his family in the midst of more than 6000% inflation in the Iraqi dinar, it was a sacrificial gift indeed. Not only that, but I am wearing a large cross around my neck, and yet he trusts me to take his gift to a Palestinian—and evidently, he believes we are going to make it there! I pray for the Lord's richest blessings upon the farmer and his family. And I pray to myself that the farmer's trust in me to make it to Palestine is how this journey will end.

We hiked a good 30 km again today and I have not had any ill effects from my gulp of water earlier in the day. Tonight will be the first night that we are camping out on the road, rather than returning to the Sagman. Our travel strategy going forward will be to travel as far as we could for any given day, then mark that spot, go back in vehicles to our previous campsite, then have vehicles take us all out to the marker where we ended our journey the previous day. After several days, the campsite will be moved several days journey ahead of where we started that day. We will caravan several days toward our campsite, and then for several days beyond our campsite, each time vehicles bringing the pilgrims forward or back to our basecamp. Using this method, the crew only had to dissemble and reassemble our basecamp every 5 or 6 days (with a few smaller sleeping tents, and a large Bedouin tent for meals!). The crew will not actually be roughing it. We have been supplied with fresh water tanks, lighted toilet, lighted tents, with beds and mattresses, and a shower tent. And the food is great.

Thursday, November 2nd. For the last two days we have been walking up the eastern bank of the Euphrates. Today, that is going to change. Our group crosses a long bridge welded together with thin metal planks stretching across the river, and we arrive in Heet. After several days of traveling in barren surroundings, this is a busy city. Our camels are now spooked by the traffic and the swarms of pedestrians. Here we try to keep our caravan of walkers and camels close together as we navigate our way through curving city streets.

In the middle of the city, several men in suits—local officials—meet us, and lead us down to their famous tar pits. Our suited guides tell us a bit about the history of the tar pits. In ancient times—as far back as 3000 years ago—the tar from these pits was used to caulk boats, and in building the city and paving the streets of Babylon. They wish us all the best on the rest of our journey. Upon leaving Heet, we are instantly returned to the middle of nowhere—a desert highway on the west bank of the Euphrates stretching into the horizon.

Meeting Mayor in Heet

Tar Pits of Heet With Fire

Friday, November 3rd. Today is a rest day. After a breakfast of fried eggs, Keith, Todd, Tim, and the rest of our soccer crew build a soccer pitch out in front of our campsite. Then, in the afternoon, Abu Galen, the owner of the land we are camping on, brought his kids along with a youth team from Ramadi. Good game. At halftime the score was 0-0. Unfortunately for our side, fatigue set in and the Arab young men took the game, 8-2.

Saturday, November 4th. This morning our meditation was on the 49th beautiful name of God, AL-BAITH, "The Renewer of Life". Today is George Sada's birthday. George has been a great gift to us, in helping make our Journey through Iraq possible!

Todd Elkins and George Sada
Preparing Fish Fry for George's Birthday

Fish Getting Cooked

Walking along the highway on the western bank of the Euphrates becomes more difficult, going gradually further and further uphill. Later that afternoon we came upon a crowd of people in front of a local shop. The shop owner brought out several cases of cold Pepsi and Orange Soda for everyone. After enjoying an Orange Soda and thanking the owner, Peter Ryan and I left the main caravan behind to enjoy their Sodas, and proceeded on ahead. Then gunshots of celebration were fired into the air behind us. It was unexpected, and we were a bit startled at first (to say the least), but it was actually a demonstration of great respect. This is done traditionally to mark any special event, like births or weddings—or Pilgrims like us!

Shop Keeper Welcomes Us With Sodas

But we push on for a total of 30 kilometers for the day, trying to reach the city of Baghdadi. Then, on the way back to our base, we stop by to pay our respects at a local wake, which was mourning the death of the local region's Sheikh. We enter a large hall where a number of prestigious locals in suits and Sheikhs in Arab gowns have gathered. We stand in front of a long line of chairs and couches, and after a short prayer, sit down. The curtains of the windows were flung fully open, and outside a horde of children were staring in, trying to catch a glimpse of what the men were doing in here. Peter Ryan remembers having the sudden urge to make funny faces to entertain this new audience, but thank goodness the polite sobriety required in our current surroundings outweighed any such temptations.

Once the new Sheikh had formally welcomed us, we were offered water, then tea, then coffee, then tea again. Hospitality is important on such occasions! The new Sheikh than gave a talk honoring the man who had died. A later translation of the talk was given to us for a keepsake of the occasion, as follows: "There are four kinds of people in this world. The first is the man who has both wealth and wisdom, and he spends his wealth for the good of others. This man is acceptable before God. The second man has no wealth, but has wisdom and knows that if he had wealth, he would spend it for the good of others. This man too is acceptable to God. The third man has wealth and no wisdom, and spends whatever he has selfishly. This man God does not accept. The fourth man has neither wealth nor wisdom, and if he had wealth he would spend it selfishly. Neither is he acceptable to God. Our Sheikh, who has passed away, was like the first man!"

Eventually we were invited to participate in an entire meal. The meal was served outdoors. The traditional meal served on such occasions is called a "mansaf", which is lamb over rice (with a special sauce), served on giant platters. The men stood around the tables, (with the children in a separate area, and the women out of sight), digging into the meat and rice with their right hand (only please), and making a ball with the rice, which is then popped into their mouths. Since I had been to a few other mansafs in the past, I had this technique down pretty well, but some of our Pilgrims were not so fortunate.

Mansaf Meal

96

After dinner we sat and listened to the local Imam (Muslim teacher) preach for over two hours in Arabic. Even the Arabic speakers were beginning to fall asleep. At the time, of course, some of us might have imagined the worst: that the Imam was preaching Jihad, and specifically targeting Americans (like some of us!). Later, we heard some of his speech's translation, and we realized that the Imam had some interesting things to say. For example, he commented that it doesn't matter which direction you face when you pray, as long as your heart is facing towards God. If you are not praying sincerely, then even if you are facing towards Mecca, God does not hear your prayer.

We arose shortly after the Imam finished speaking, and George and I offered a prayer and our condolences.

George and Robin Offering A Prayer

We all then head back to our basecamp. But the night wasn't over yet. It was General George Sada's birthday, and there was chocolate cake for all of us before we, at last, crept back to our beds.

George Blowing Out Candles
On His Birthday Cake

Sunday, November 5th. Today our caravan left from Baghdadi and walked through the desert all day toward Haditha. I was not feeling well today, and my feet were feeling worse, and I fell farther and farther behind the main group. At the end of the day I decided to go back to Baghdad one more time with George Sada. First of all, we wanted to get a final answer on whether we had permission to continue to the border. Second, I needed to find a new pair of shoes that would make walking less painful.

Evidently, I missed out on a giant "farewell" party thrown by Abu Galen, who had generously allowed us to set up our present camp on his property. He hired a singer and keyboardist, and a large number of people (all men) came from the surrounding villages to listen to the music and dance.

Crowd Gathering at Abu Galen Farewell Party

As Jason Drake described the evening in his journal, "the music was loud and very Arab, with a crowd of about 300 men jumping, dancing and carrying on." Our Pilgrims were seated as guests of honor in plastic chairs on the edge of the dance floor, and some were pulled out onto the dance floor to take part in the festive "dancing". Peter Ryan, with his sore, blistered feet, eventually wrapped his arms around his chair's arms to avoid being pulled out into the action.

Monday, November 6th. This morning we get the final permission we need to go all the way to the border with Syria. George Sada called ahead to the support crew and said that tomorrow morning, after the caravan gets on the road, they should move the basecamp forward several days.

And after hunting far and wide in Baghdad, I did somehow find a pair of size 14 tennis shoes! I doubt that they really are size 14's in American sizes, but they are large enough for me to wrap my feet in bandages, and wear several pairs of heavy wool socks over the bandages to cushion my feet. Since I am missing a day of walking, I will have to walk double the distance tomorrow, but it is worth it to have finally found a good pair of shoes!

Meanwhile, our caravan of Pilgrims and camels got out on the empty stretch of highway and headed north. According to Peter Ryan's diary, after a long day of walking, they drove around scouting out several cities in the area to find a local restaurant with enough food to feed the whole group. They finally found a place in the city of Rawa, that had a whole lamb hanging from a hook out front, which Peter described as "drawing us in like a dangling fisherman's lure". After a satisfying meal, Keith and Prosper continued their new tradition of tossing out small candies to the children that gathered around their vehicle as they pulled away. Eventually our Pilgrims found their way to the new campsite, where four Bedouin tents had been set up on a patch of cornfield that overlooked the Euphrates. Peter tells us that at night "the river is lit by a dozen sparkling rubies" (the lights of fisherman's boats).

Tuesday, November 7th. Today the 52nd name of the 99 names of God is AL-WAKIL, "The One Who Gives Us Strength". We find this in our New Testament, where Paul declares in Philippians 4:13, "I can do all things through Christ who gives me strength."

Just what I need to hear as I get out on the road at 6 AM to start at the spot I had marked at the end of the day on November 5th. I had a lot of catching up to do—two days walk in one day! Could I do that? Really? Up at their new campsite, our caravan of Pilgrims had a relaxed morning. They slept in, and then had a substantial breakfast of eggs and bread, and a platter of fried onions and tomatoes. Evidently they thought that they were going to get a rest day while waiting for me to catch up. So they were not happy when Edward's car came tearing into camp and let them know they were supposed to be out on the highway moving forward. They were soon out on the road, a day spent completely in the desert—no homes or buildings or water—just some occasional sheep herds, telephone lines and "endless road", as Peter Ryan described it.

My day looks exactly the same. No distractions. Just desert and the road ahead as far as one could see. But my new tennis shoes, with my feet all bandaged up, are great so far! However, George Sada reminded me recently of an episode that happened to me about half way through my day. I guess I was concentrating so fiercely on covering as much ground as possible that this particular "interruption" didn't even register in my memory. George had left Baghdad later that morning and was driving hard to catch up with me, when he found me standing on the side of the road with a man holding a gun to my chest. The man was no doubt a shepherd, and when he found me out in the middle of no-where (with a cross around my neck), he figured that I must be some kind of foreign (perhaps American) spy.

George jumped out of his car and explained to the shepherd that Sadaam Hussein, himself, had actually given us permission to do our Pilgrimage. Hearing this, the shepherd became quite frightened. George said the shepherd began to shake with fear, and immediately fell on his knees in front of me and tried to kiss my feet. George said I pulled the shepherd up by his arm, and told him "mallesh!" (no problem, you're forgiven). Then George explained to him a bit more about the purpose of our Pilgrimage, and I shook the shepherd's hand, and then turned and continued on up the road. As I said at the beginning of the day, I had a lot of catching up to do!

I keep walking today until just about 8:30 P.M., or a little after, when at last I arrive at the spot where the main caravan had stopped for the day a few hours earlier. I have walked about 55 km for the day. And would you believe it, thanks to my size 14 tennis shoes my feet are fine! After this day, I think I am beginning to gain some believers that the "old man" (me) will actually be able to walk every foot of the entire journey.

Wednesday, November 8th. We are now walking along the left side of the highway, across a vast stretch of desert. The only distractions are the many oil trucks driving north on the highway toward the Syrian border, or driving south on the highway returning to pick up another load of oil. The drivers evidently have heard about our Pilgrimage, and the drivers going south beep their horns in "salute" as they pass me. All day long I raise my right arm and salute them back.

Peter Ryan's diary from this day perhaps best describes the desolation and monotony of walking up this highway in this heat. "After several weeks of walking, the road seems like home and everything else, the campsite, the meals, the towns we've left behind, begin to fade like a roll of film exposed to the sunlight. It's as if we have always been walking, since the beginning of time, and will continue to walk until the day that we die. Even when I stop for a moment, the desert keeps moving—a trick played on my eyes by the heat—stretching ahead of me like the tide of the ocean, curving deeper and deeper into the horizon, leaving me a bit sea-sick and slightly off kilter….At the moment, I am laying in my bed at our campsite, typing these words onto a computer screen, but it feels like I'm still moving, walking across the desert, inching closer and closer to our final destination."

Vast Desolation in the Desert

Thursday, November 9th. Another day of monotony, walking in the heat heading north. There are no villages to distract us—just endless desert, and the road disappearing into the horizon. These past few days I have had a lot of time to think about how much I miss my wife Nancy. It has now been 21 days since I had to say goodbye to her, and let her go back home to the U.S. by herself. I realize that the Iraqi government was just using an abundance of caution in requiring her to be sent back, but the Iraqi people have been more than wonderful to us every day, in every way, everywhere. Nancy could have been with me this whole trip through Iraq, and been having a wonderful time. She would have loved it all.

I spend the whole day saluting the drivers in the oil trucks as they drive by beeping their horns, until my right arm begins to stiffen up. Finally, toward the end of the day, a truck driver pulls off the road in front of me and comes to talk with me. He is very friendly, and in halting English (but far better than any of my Arabic!) he asks me to explain to him what we are doing out here in the middle of no-where. I do my best with some memorized phrases in Arabic to tell him that I am a "messiah" ("Christian" in Arabic, which is pretty obvious by the large cross I am wearing around my neck), and that we are traveling (God willing) to Bethlehem to honor Jesus on his 2000th birthday. Jesus is called the "Prince of Peace", so on our way we are praying a blessing upon all the people we pass—for them, and their families, and their homes and fields and animals. The truck driver nods his head in approval, and declares, "you are a Muslim!" I assume that I wasn't fully understood the first time, so I try again. And the truck driver smiles warmly, nods his head up and down in approval, shakes my hand, and again pronounces, "you are a Muslim!" Then he returns to his truck, beeps his horn in salute, and drives on down the road. I reflect on the meaning of this encounter for the next few miles as I finish the day's walk. I conclude that he is doing his best to honor me, and with the only language he has to explain it, he is telling me that he sees me as "a servant of God".

Friday, November 10th. Thank goodness, today is a rest day. General George Sada, to help celebrate our upcoming departure from Iraq, has brought a dozen young Assyrian Christians from Baghdad. Ten of them—evenly divided between men and women—dress in traditional Assyrian costumes and perform a dance for us, while two older men play a Zora (a strange mix between a trumpet and a flute), and a Dahoola (a type of drum). Several of the lovely young women are George Sada's nieces, so our whole crew of young men are cautioned by George to be on their best behavior!

Assyrian Dancers

Assyrian Dancers with Pilgrim Crew

Saturday, November 11th. Today we are heading for the city of al-Qaim, which sits just below the border with Syria. At the beginning of the day, Khalid, Oday, Sagben and Sagmon (our four Shite Muslim camel handlers) come up to us, and ask if they could please borrow our three staffs fashioned into crosses. We aren't sure what was going on, but agree to hand them over. Then three of them walk out in front of our caravan carrying the crosses over their heads. The fourth camel handler walks just in front of them, and begins chanting from an Arabic gospel of John. They march in this formation all the way through the city of al-Qaim. To say the least, we are astonished. At the very least, it is their way of expressing their appreciation for our crew, and for our Pilgrimage of prayer, seeking peace for the people of Iraq. Their clothing would undoubtedly identify them as Shite Muslims, so I think it was very courageous of them to march through the city carrying crosses on our behalf.

Phil Elkins, our expedition coordinator, was finally able to join us on our last day in Iraq. He had planned to be here much earlier, to be part of our whole journey through Iraq. But his mother had grown very ill down in Abilene, Texas, and Phil had gone down there to be with her. On October 16th she finally went home to the Lord.

Phil came down with Souhel Daas, our Journey coordinator. who would mange our travels through Syria. Through Souhel's contacts at the border, Phil was able to locate us at our last campsite in Iraq, and was able to come across and join us in Iraq for one day. He shared with us the good news that sufficient arrangements had been made for our traveling through Syria, and that our new support team was waiting for us on the other side of the border in Abu Kamal, with fresh camels and supplies. In each new country we crossed into it was necessary to change camels, because it was not allowable to bring camels across national borders. Our new support team, with Souhel and several other members of a Muslim tribal group from Palmyra, would support us with camels and tents and meals from here to the Jordanian border.

Sunday, November 12th. Our devotions today begin with the 57th of the 99 beautiful names of God: AL-MUHSI, "The Reconciler". We walk the final 10 or 12 km to the border trying to stay together as a group. Our Iraqi support crew, including Edward, Solomon, and Albert, and the Iraqi security men walk along with us. As we approach the Iraqi border station, we say our final goodbyes. There are more than a few tears, requests for prayer (even from the Iraqi security men), and many hugs—all very emotionally intense. Having spent 22 days together sharing our meals, our pains, and our triumphs (we made it through another day!), we have become like family with so many of our support crew, including our Iraqi security detail and our camel handlers.

Prayer at the Iraqi Border with Phil Elkins

At the border security on the Iraqi side of the border, we had to wait for governmental clearance for our "internationals", John (the Philippines), Prosper (Zimbabwe), and Keith (England). Keith's visa, which had to be reissued on the spot, ended up causing the most difficulties, and Prosper stayed back there with him to offer moral support, even though he had already been cleared. The rest of our Pilgrims searched for small patches of shade on the curbs and patiently waited (or not) for the rest of our team members. Thanks to Souhel Daas, we were able to resolve the customs issues, and Keith was finally cleared to enter Syria.

We pass through a set of roadblocks and enter the Syrian border station. A sign proclaims, "Welcome to Syria: The Cradle of Civilization". We go in to fill out more forms. All our equipment and our three "internationals" are graciously given permission to enter Syria. We present a few officials with soccer balls as a token of our appreciation, board the vans provided by Souhel Daas, and drive through Abu Kamal toward our campsite near Dura-Europos. All our delay at the border has made it too late in the day to try to walk and ride camels from the border up to our campsite near Dura-Europos. In the morning we will get back in the vans and return to the border, pick up our camels, and start walking and riding to reach Dura-Europos.

CHAPTER THREE

CARAVANING THROUGH SYRIA

As we would soon learn, our new support team leader is the truly amazing Souhel Daas. For the next 29 days and many hundreds of miles, wherever we were, and whatever problems we might encounter, Souhel would say, "No problem! I have a cousin down the road who will be able to help us with that". And he did! Our campsite near by Dura-Europos consisted of one large Bedouin tent where we had our meals morning and evening, and four smaller tents for sleeping.

Monday, November 13th. The old city of Dura-Europos probably dates back to at least 300 B.C. It sits up on an escarpment about 90 meters (300 ft) above the Euphrates. It was once the location of one of the oldest Christian churches in the world, possibly dating back as far as 100 A.D., although it was probably just a "house church" that met in a larger complex of buildings. The surviving frescoes of a room that would later serve as the baptistery—"The Good Shepherd", "The Healing of the Paralytic", and "Christ and Peter Walking on Water"— are considered by some to be the earliest known depictions of Jesus Christ, perhaps dating as early as 235 A.D.

We are driven back to just beyond the Syrian border station, and are now headed back toward Dura-Europos, traveling up the highway on the west bank of the Euphrates. On the Magi's original journey, Dura-

Europos is where they would have crossed over from the east bank to the west bank of the Euphrates—probably on some sort of raft—on their way (across many miles of desert) to the oasis city of Palmyra. The modern day highway no longer made it possible to go up the Euphrates on the east bank. This was one of the rare places on our reenactment that for a few miles we were not able to follow precisely in the Magi's footsteps (or camel hoof prints!).

Andre and Jake Martinez, I am told later, have an interesting morning. As the core of our media crew, I had sent them ahead of the caravan to get some footage as the camels passed through Abu Kamal. They found a corner in the middle of town where there were tons of people, and classic narrow Middle Eastern streets with vendors and goods laid out. Andre even got up on the roof of a two story building, being a perfect spot to catch the camels come around the corner and down the street. When they turned another corner onto the main street, Jake would be set up with his camera. They were waiting for the camels for about 15-20 minutes, and a large number of children began to gather around Jake on the main street. Finally a person dressed in plain clothes came over to Jake and announced, "police", and grabbed his camera. Jake tried to stand his ground, until the man again said "police', and pointed over to a uniformed man who was heading toward Jake. Then the two officers began walking Jake across the street toward the nearby police station.

Meanwhile, Andre was shooting some footage from the rooftop, and didn't see what was happening to Jake, but the police motioned to Andre to come down also. While Andre was packing up his camera equipment, Phil Elkins and Souhel Daas come walking down the street and spot Andre, and Andre tells them that Jake is over at the police station.

Souhel goes over and talks to the police for a spell, and then the police take everyone inside the police station. Turns out that a call to the mayor's office of the city reveals that the mayor has a paper on his desk giving the media team permission to be there and take photos. So everything is fine—then tea is ordered for everyone! Whew!

Walking along by myself that afternoon I saw the most amazing site. Off to my right in the desert, traveling in the opposite direction of our caravan, was a young Bedouin girl of perhaps 12, riding side-saddle on her donkey. She had the most amazing bright blue eyes and beautiful red hair. I later ask Souhel to explain to me how this could be, and he said, "Crusader child!". The last Crusade was more than 700 years ago. Evidently a few crusaders settled down in the area after one of their Crusades and took a Bedouin wife. DNA is a powerful thing. More than 700 years later, the Crusader's prodigy is still obvious.

Today is my 59th birthday, but whose counting? Everyone is too tired to party. Jason Drake spends the evening trying to solve technical problems for everyone. He gets our satellite phone up and running, so we could stay in touch with Sami in Palestine, George Halley (our communications expert) in Pasadena, California, and whomever else we will need to be in touch with in the days ahead.

Tuesday, November 14th. Today Jason has to stay behind at our basecamp and try to straighten out some things that got messed up on our website. The rest of us head west out into the vast desert expanse that lies between Dura-Europos and Palmyra. Toward the end of our day's hike, we see an unrecognizable figure off in the distance. Soon he is greeting us, and we realize that it is Peter Thiep, our friend from South Sudan, who has at long last joined us on our Pilgrimage. Because of his refugee status, Peter was denied entry into Iraq, and had been waiting patiently in Amman, Jordan for a chance to join us in Syria.

Peter will be our fourth Magi, so after a brief bite to eat back at our campsite, the whole group wanders over to the nearby ruins of Dura-Europos, whose huge city walls contain the barely visible remains of a

Greek-style amphitheater. As the sun begins to set, the media crew has everyone get into their costumes, and film several scenes in the ruins to capture Peter Thiep, our newest wise man, greeting his comrades and joining them in their walk through the desert toward Bethlehem in search for the new born King.

Jason Drake has to stay at basecamp another day to solve various electronic problems. He spends the day trying to piece his computer together after receiving a virus from who knows where. He said it feels "surreal"—sitting in the middle of nowhere in the Syrian desert talking to our tech wizard George Halley in the U.S. on the satellite phone, while simultaneously using another computer to check things on the internet on another satellite phone, and so on throughout the day. Still not sure how Phil Elkins managed to recruit such an awesome crew of Pilgrims with the technical skills needed, along with the personal resolve to stay on the problem until it is solved. With the Lord's help no doubt. They are an amazing bunch of Pilgrims.

Meanwhile, I was out early this morning about 6:30 AM continuing to walk west across the desert toward Palmyra. We might still be 7 or 8 days from reaching Palmyra. The rest of our caravan crew got out on the road (not an actual road—just desert gravel and sand) about 7:30, and eventually caught up with me. The new camels we picked up in Syria move a lot faster than the camels we had earlier in Iraq. So this should help us travel farther and make better time doing it. They also seem to be generally healthier, and consistently friendlier to humans. But some of the caravan crew have told me that riding on a camel, in addition to inducing vertigo, produces a severe sense of powerlessness. The camel, at all times, is in control! Peter Thiep, after taking his first ride on one of the camels earlier today, seems to agree. "I feel better now that I am walking", he reports to Peter Ryan, as the camels race on ahead of us.

Since we got an early start this morning, after 35 kilometers we pull over in some shade and call it quits. We enjoy a few cheese sandwiches, and after sharing the leftover remains of tomatoes and rolls with our new pets, the vans take us back to our basecamp near Dura-Europos. Tonight I get the wonderful news that my wife Nancy arrived in Damascus yesterday, and will be heading for Palmyra tomorrow. Tomorrow, after we get moving out on the desert, they plan to move our basecamp about three days ahead to near T2, a petroleum plant in the middle of nowhere.

Thursday, November 16th. Even out here, deep within the void of the Syrian desert, our caravan crew are buzzing with the news about the U.S. Presidential elections (thanks to our hard working media team). It seems as though Gore, after a recount, may have won, after Bush was originally thought to be the victor. I guess we will have to stay tuned a little longer for the final outcome.

Tonight, Prosper, Keith, John and Jake went with the chief of police at T2 (a petroleum plant) to watch Champion League Football (soccer). Someone at the plant had Sky TV, and let them come and watch. He spoke pretty good English, so they were able to tell him about the purpose of our journey. While watching the game, they were served chai (tea), along with oranges and bananas. There is a lot we in America could learn from the Syrian people's practice of hospitality. But guys, never mind the football score, was there any more news about the U.S. election?

Friday, November 17th. I walk with renewed urgency today, and wanted to cover as many kilometers as possible, because even though we are still a number of days away from Palmyra, tonight I am going to have a van drive me to the Cham Palace Hotel in Palmyra to meet my missing wife!

That evening I wind up taking Todd Elkins and Peter Thiep along with me. As it turns out, we picked a good night to be in a hotel. I learn the next day that it rained all Friday night, and that holes began to appear in some of our tents. They had to pile raincoats over their sleeping bags throughout the night, and move into the center of their tents. Finally, Jason, Jake and Andre all moved into my empty tent. They learned from Andre Martinez that night that he was writing a song about our last days in Iraq and our first few days in Syria. We are all looking forward to hearing it somewhere down the road.

Saturday, November 18th. I am driven this morning the long way around back to where I stopped last night, because a bridge, which had been under construction to cross Wadi al Miyah, has been washed away by a flash flood overnight. When I catch up with our Pilgrims, we spend some time in the morning at that very bridge. It's ironic that here in the middle of a barren desert the thing that stops our progress is water. This is the rain we have been praying for, but in the desert, evidently, when it rains, "it pours"! For several hours there was no way to pass for people, cars or camels. Finally, someone came with a bulldozer and plowed piles of dirt to make a temporary bridge so we could get under way again.

We Prayed for Rain and We Got It!

Crossing Wadi On Temporary Fill

Robin Thanking Truck Driver

At the end of the day I had a van bring me back to my wife at the Cham Palace Hotel. Later that night several of our crew couldn't find their campsite in the dark, and stumbled into some strangers Bedouin tent, so they decided to have the van just bring them to join me and Nancy at the Cham Palace Hotel. At least that was their story!

Sunday, November 19th. Our meditation for the day is on the 64th name of God's 99 beautiful names—AL-WAJID, "The One Who Finds Us" (no matter where we are!).

We spend some time thanking the Lord for the rain we had been praying for, for several weeks, on behalf of the Iraqi and Syrian people. And as part of our devotions, Andre sings the song he has written expressing our hopes and doubts on the journey thus far:

DEEPER

From the city streets filled with bricks and mud
    Where the smoke can tear your eyes
To the barren bends of desolation road
    Where the earth is cracked and dry
And all these faces passing by
    Some with carpets at your feet
And others with their shy reply
    Squinted glances through the trees
WE MUST TAKE IT DEEPER
    THROUGH THESE CRUSTED EYES
WE MUST TAKE IT DEEPER
    TO WHERE THE SPIRIT LIES
Is there any merit
    In the blisters on our feet?
The sure pace of this desert train
    All the miles in this heat?
Oh, can we scrape an ounce of hope
    Or wave a sprig of peace?

Is it all just desert dust
    Swirling in the breeze?
WE MUST TAKE IT DEEPER
    THROUGH THESE CRUSTED EYES
WE MUST TAKE IT DEEPER
    TO WHERE THE SPIRIT LIES
WE MUST TAKE IT DEEPER
    THROUGH THESE CRUSTED EYES
PAST ALL THE POLITICS
    THE RHETORIC AND LIES
YEAH, WE MUST TAKE IT DEEPER
    WHERE THE WELL NEVER RUNS DRY
WE MUST TAKE IT DEEPER
    TO WHERE THE SPIRIT LIES

Copyright 2000 Andre K. Martinez

My prayer following Andre's song: "We thank you, Lord, for our brother Andre's gifts for words and song. And we pray today that all the blisters on our feet will somehow, by God's grace, translate into blessings for all the people we pass by, and one day mean something for the cause of peace throughout the Middle East. Amen."

Following our meditation, we plod another 35 kilometers through the desert heat. Thanks to Jason (and all the rest of the media support team) we now are able to connect with Sami Awad in Palestine. The news is not good. During the first month of the Second Intifada (September 28th through October), 144 Palestinians were killed and 5984 wounded. During this same period there were 12 Israeli's killed and 65 wounded. Clashes have been continuing every day there in November thus far, with Palestinians being killed and wounded at about the same rate as the previous month. Alarming! Will we actually be able to enter Palestine when (and if) we finally get there? Will there even be a Christmas in Bethlehem this year? But Sami Awad tells us, "keep on coming!"

We have not yet officially reached the city of Palmyra by walking, but after another long hiking day the whole Pilgrim crew will travel by the vans and join Nancy and I at the Cham Palace Hotel.

Monday, November 20th. I had a fever last night, and Nancy convinced me to give everybody a well-deserved rest day today (wives have a way of being very convincing). Just across the road from the Hotel are the magnificent ancient ruins of Palmyra. When the original Magi passed through here in perhaps late 5 B.C., it was an important and essential oasis providing the way across the vast desert for caravans traveling from Persia to Rome and Egypt.

Ruins of Palmyra

By the 2nd and 3rd Century A.D. the Palmyrenes had become renowned as merchants. Their significant wealth enabled them to construct monumental projects such as the Great Colonnade, The Temple of Bel, and the tower tombs. The Temple of Bel was at that time consecrated to the Mesopotamian god, Bel. The inhabitants during this time were largely Amorites, Arameans, and Arabs, and they at that time spoke a dialect of Aramaic, while using Greek for commerce and diplomatic purposes.

By the late 4th Century A.D., the majority of the inhabitants had converted to Christianity, and by the mid-6th Century the Temple of Bel had been converted to a Christian Church. Then, by the late 7th Century, the region was conquered by Islam, and Arabic became the dominate spoken language, as it is today.

Our Pilgrim crew toured the extensive ruins. The walls of the ancient city extended outward 6 kilometers, with a second wall extending another 20. Pillars throughout the city have platforms where thousands of statues once stood to honor heroic soldiers, rich merchants, and the noble class, many of which are now held in the Palmyra museum. The highlight of our tour (at least for Peter Ryan) was the "funerary towers"—a number of five story towers, which at one point housed 200-400 coffins. Rather than burying their dead in the ground, the Palmyrenes buried them in the sky. The ancient city also had a small Greek-style outdoor theater, a series of baths for bathing, and even an underground sewage system. The ruins of Palmyra were designated a UNESCO World Heritage site in 1980.

My wife Nancy has been here in Palmyra since November 17th. I am very grateful for the Moafak Daas family, who have shown my wife such warm hospitality while I am out trudging across the desert. Moafak Daas is the brother of Souhel Daas, and runs the Daas Bazar, a store in Palmyra that seems to have a little bit of everything, including jewelry, rugs, you name it. Moafak has 4 children. Three boys (Salman, Ahmad, and Mohammad) and a young girl named Lamaa (sometimes called LuLu). Nancy loves children, so she has enjoyed spending time with them all. She especially has enjoyed holding LuLu in her lap while LuLu shows Nancy her school work. This is all in Arabic of course, which Nancy does not speak. But LuLu is very excited about school, and about her homework, and this comes through very clearly.

Somehow Nancy manages to communicate to LuLu how proud she is of LuLu's schoolwork, and they have a wonderful time together!

Moafak Daas and Wife in Front of Their Bazar

Tuesday, November 21st. I am still recovering from a touch of something like the flu, so everyone gets to sleep in, and have another day off. Later that morning everyone got fitted for some sheepskin coats that Nancy is having made for the entire Pilgrim crew. While we had some pretty hot weather trudging through the desert in the past week, the nights in the desert are beginning to grow cold. Nancy also got these same people to work on making flags and banners for **Journey of the Magi 2000: A Pilgrimage for Peace.** She also came up with another great idea—a special banner that we will hold aloft when we march through the streets, God willing, from Shepherds Field to Manger Square on

Christmas Day. When it is ready we will get to see her surprise gift to the Palestinian people.

Everyone came back to the hotel for lunch, but Jake, Tim, Andre and Keith ordered room service, and stayed back in their rooms to work on editing clips. After lunch Peter Ryan, Prosper, John Vencer and Peter Thiep, along with Gasan (our new Palestinian camera man), were invited next door for tea with Adnan Khatib, the head manager of the agency of news and radio in Palmyra. Even before tea had been served, Adnan was quick to extract some information from the group. "First", he said in Arabic, which was then translated, "give your names and occupations. Then tell me the purpose behind the journey, and what you have thought, so far, of Syria".

They were not really prepared for an interview, but John Vencer came through with a detailed response. "The main purpose of our reenactment of the Journey of the Magi, apart from retracing the route of the Wise Men from the Bible, is to put a face on the people of the Middle East, and especially in the areas we are traveling through. From the International News media in the U.S., mostly the only news people get about the Middle East is negative news. Many people end up believing that all Middle Easterners are terrorists. But we want to show people here as they really are: they are the same as us. They love their children and we love our children. They wake up and go to work every morning just like we do."

Peter Thiep then explained to the radio host our journey's personal meaning to him. "The purpose of our journey is to find peace between Muslims and Christians. I am from South Sudan, where they are at war, so I am here on this journey to say we need peace for everyone. We need peace for Sudan, and peace between Islam and Christianity." When I heard about their meeting, and the responses of John and Peter, I was very proud of them for doing such a good job in representing all of us on the journey.

Wednesday, November 22nd. After two days rest, we hike a good forty kilometers through more sparse desert wasteland. But we have almost pushed through the most barren section of our journey. Tomorrow we should be finally arriving on the outskirts of Palmyra. At the end of the day today, before going back to the Cham Palace Hotel, we all stop by our new basecamp outside Palmyra, where the camels and our support crew are staying, and Nancy joins us there.

Taking off our shoes, we enter the large Bedouin tent where a fire and cushions had been prepared for us. We are met with seven new faces staring back at us. They are all brothers—perhaps elementary school age and even a few younger. Just before we arrived they had come to the tent for an unexpected visit. Our generous host, Souhel Daas, asked them why they had come, and they replied, "to take some rest here with you." But I am sure they were hoping for more than that, and soon their hopes were fulfilled with a plastic bag filled with fruit to take home to their mother, and their hands full of cookies. We learned that the children were fatherless, and were out in the desert tending perhaps a 150 sheep.

Before long, one of the Palmyra support team started beating a drum, and Souhel and others started dancing. They pulled Prosper and Peter Thiep into the fray, and also tried to convince the shy brothers to join them on the dance floor. While dancing, they also made up a special song just for my lovely wife Nancy—about how many camels I had to give her father as the bride price in order to marry her. First it was 50 camels, then 75, then 100 camels, and so on—the price grew larger as the night progressed. Nancy of course loved watching all the dancing, and the song made up especially for her!

Thursday, November 23rd. Thanksgiving day in the U.S.! Unfortunately, it is not likely that there are any turkeys out here for a Thanksgiving dinner. We arrive at the outskirts of the city in the late afternoon. We prepare for our arrival into the city by draping a series of flags across the saddles of our camels (British, Syrian, Iraqi, Sudanese, Palestinian, and American). And we have our four Magi dress up in their costumes.

Our Magi Riding into Palmyra

Soon we arrive into the city itself, where large crowds of people await us. Swarms of children begin running excitedly beside us. Several are so excited that they accidentally pull Prosper off his camel (he survives without injury). Nancy joins me on the outskirts of the city, and together we walk through the city proper. A young boy of about 10 or 12 comes out of the crowd and walks up to Nancy and offers his arm to her—quite the gentleman! He proudly walks Nancy most of the way through the city, until we approach our hotel.

Young Boy Escorts Nancy Through Palmyra

Journey Caravan at the Ruins of Palmyra

FOOTNOTE: While writing this book some 20 years later, this past week we were remembering this young boy and also LuLu, and we prayed at lunchtime that we might somehow be able to be in touch with them. To be honest, I was very much in doubt that this would be possible. But by the afternoon I found myself in touch with both of them! I had already been connected with one of Souhel Daas's nephews, Yousef Daas, who was helping me stay up to date with Souhel. When I described to him some of my wife's favorite memories about our journey through Palmyra, including the young boy who took her by the arm and walked her through the city, he responded, "that was me!" He was 12 years old and he remembers it well, and also about going out to our Journey's next base camp a few days later, where he played soccer with our soccer crew. He also put me in touch with Lamaa (LuLu), and we have been emailing with her this week! Nancy is beside herself with happiness!

As we neared the Cham Palace hotel, a stream of people came walking down the road in the opposite direction, heading for the center of the city. It turns out that they were prisoners who had just been released from prison—perhaps as a traditional gesture that is done in preparation for the approach of Ramadan. One young man in the group was obviously badly impaired—probably a victim of polio or some other affliction. Was he in prison because of some illegal behavior—or just because of his affliction? My guess is that it was the later. But in any case, he saw me—dressed in white with a long flowing beard—and must have decided that I was a Hajji. Perhaps he thought that if he could reach me, he could receive a badly needed blessing. Whatever his reason, he was determined to reach me, but other prisoners began to slap him in the head, and sought to steer him away from getting to me. But there was no stopping him. He staggered forward to receive a blessing from what he understood to be a Holy Man. He reached out his arms to embrace me. Unfortunately, it was just me—the all too human Robin Wainwright. But as the large crowd of prisoners rushed by, I was able to reach out and embrace the young man, and whisper an Arabic blessing in his ear. Then he was pulled away from me by the other prisoners, and the band of prisoners hurried on past us. I have often thought of this young man in the years following this event, and have continued to pray that somehow our merciful God would bless him far beyond anything I was able to give him. Shortly after this encounter, we reach the Cham Palace Hotel, and the rest of the caravan crew join me and Nancy there for dinner.

Friday, November 24th. For the next section of our journey, we are leaving the road in order to follow the actual route taken by the original Magi. Most of the time, today's roads do follow the path of ancient caravan trails, but here the ruins of ancient caravansaries—places where in earlier times camels and people could find shelter and food—testify to the true location of the ancient caravan route. So today, where the road turns left and south, the original caravan route went straight ahead, passing through the valley at the foot of Jabal al Busayri. However, over time the "path" had become strewn with everything from small pebbles to large boulders, which makes our traveling difficult.

At one point John Vencer's camel stumbled on a boulder going up a ravine. The camel, Gazella, as our crew called her, sat down and refused to move any further. Eventually, our camel handlers determined that none of her legs were injured, and they tried to yank her into standing up. This didn't work so well, so finally the camel handlers and our caravan crew lured Gazella into standing up with chunks from an orange. Once she was up on all fours, she was fine with moving forward, and we all began moving again. We ended the day early, and our soccer crew rushed off in a van to compete in a soccer match back in Palmyra. They won a trophy, which they presented to Nancy, naming her the "General Manager" of the Magi 2000 soccer team.

Saturday, November 25th. This morning our Pilgrim crew leaves the Cham Palace Hotel for the last time, and our basecamp is moved several days ahead of us to the ruins of Halabat. I go with them for the first part of the day. We are soon met with a swarm of reporters from Reuters, Associated Press, and other news agencies from Syria. After completing the interviews, I meet up with some Bedouin families with children who have come out to see us.

Robin Giving Some Fruit to the Children

By around noon a van takes me back to the Cham Palace, where Nuhad Tomeh has come to take me and Nancy to the village of Al Hafar. The Presbyterian Church there is the home church of Rev. Dr. Riad Jarjour, who is currently the General Secretary of the Middle East Council of Churches in Beirut, Lebanon. This is the Christian village where Nancy's mother helped provide some of the funds to dig the village well deeper—from 300 ft. to 1200 ft.—another example of our "gifts of the Magi" for **The Journey of the Magi 2000: A Pilgrimage for Peace**. The well serves not only the Christian portion of the village, but Muslim farmers as well—a demonstration of the compassion of Jesus intended for all peo*ple.*

Several vans pick up the rest of our Pilgrim crew about 1:30 p.m. to bring them to meet Nancy and I at the village of Al Hafar. Unfortunately, the vans get lost and what was supposed to be an hour's trip takes almost three hours.

When Nancy and I arrive with Nuhad Tomeh on time at Al Hafer, Dr. Riad Jarjour is there to meet us. Riad's little Presbyterian Church has prepared a special banquet for us. Many of the people of the village wait patiently for the arrival our Pilgrims, and greet them warmly when their vans finally pull into the driveway.

Riad has arranged for Father Abdullah, from the Syrian Orthodox Church, to provide a welcoming speech for us: "In the name of our two Christian villages, Hafar and Sadad, and in the name of our fathers, we welcome you. We hope that your objectives and goals will be achieved, and that you will each go back to your homes safely. We also ask that you pray for us when you get to Bethlehem, in the place where salvation was offered to all, since we cannot go there ourselves. So especially pray for us when you reach Bethlehem."

Prayer Service at Al Hafar

I respond to his greeting with an apology for our tardiness, a promise that we would indeed pray for their communities when we reach Bethlehem, and a request that they pray for us as we continue on our way there. Then four of the church leaders sing a prayer in Aramaic, in four-part harmony, which is quite beautiful and reminiscent of Gregorian chants. After the musical prayer, we all sit down to a fine meal of Safiha—which is a Syrian meat pie made by making a bowl of bread, and then filling it with meat, onions, tomatoes, pine nuts, and spices, and served with a bowl of yogurt, as well as fresh fruit for dessert (when I get home, I am really going to miss Middle Eastern food!).

Pilgrims Being Served a Meal in Al Hafar

After the meal, I thank our hosts, and Nancy and I return to Palmyra with Nuhad Tomeh, while the Pilgrim crew drive out to their new basecamp at the ruins of Halabat.

Sunday, November 26th. The car that was supposed to pick me up from the Cham Palace Hotel to take me out to meet up with the Pilgrim caravan did not show up. Our crew had a leisurely breakfast, and while waiting for me, made a brief tour of the ruins of Halabat, the crumbling remains of an old military garrison. Eventually, because of the late start, I sent back word that they should take the day off. However, they decided to go ahead and get a few miles in, and take the following day off to wait for me to catch up with them.

As described in Peter Ryan's journal, the route ahead continued to provide rocks and ravines as obstacles to slow their progress. However, clouds provided the terrain with deep shadows, providing welcome shade and a cool breeze. Toward the end of a short day of walking, however, they ran into a large rock quarry. There were endless piles of white rocks, with huge trucks roaming the quarry roads with tires taller than their drivers, and several large industrial buildings puffing smoke. Peter, Keith, Tim, Jake, and Peter Thiep all stopped off at the guard station to find out if they were even allowed to pass through the area.

With Peter Thiep acting as a translator, they learned that their friendly host sleeps in his guard station throughout the week, only going home to see his wife and seven children on Fridays. The guard station was a simple small room made from concrete with a rusty tin stove and furnace in the center of the room, and a bed in the corner. Despite the austerity of his situation, the guard said that he enjoyed his job, and offered everyone tea while they waited for a few of the others to catch up with them. When the others arrived, the guard gave them instructions on how to pass through the quarry safely. Once they were clear of the area, the sunlight had begun to fade, so they were forced to stop for the day. They hopped into the vans and returned to their new camp at Halabat.

Monday, November 27th. Today was the first day of Ramadan, the Muslim holy month. Muslims fast from sunrise to sunset, which includes refraining from both food and water. The usual pattern is to enjoy a generous breakfast well before sunrise. The fast is then broken after sunset with a light snack, to be followed by special prayers—then a celebratory dinner with family and friends later in the evening. One of the spiritual purposes of the fast of Ramadan is to remember what it feels like to be hungry or thirsty, so one will feel compassion for the poor and needy. However, those on a hajj (pilgrimage) are exempted from having to fast from either food or water. Out of respect for our hosts, including our Muslim support crew and camel handlers, many of our Pilgrims try to fast during the day anyway, although it was necessary to drink plenty of water when walking.

Our media team had a "anti-media day" today, as Andre termed it. They hadn't really had a day off for more than a month, since even on days off they are busy filming, editing, and uploading material to our website. So today they rode with one of the van drivers into Damascus for a true day off.

Meanwhile, back in Palmyra, Nancy and I spent time saying goodbye to our many new friends and hosts in Palmyra. Souhel Daas's brother, Moafak Daas, and his four children, and a handful of other children who were relatives of Souhel and Moafak, had entertained Nancy for a number of days while the rest of us were slowly working our way toward Palmyra. So today all the children stood in a line in order to, one by one, hug Nancy and kiss her goodbye. This was one of the highlights of the whole journey for Nancy.

Tuesday, November 28th. Early this morning Peter Ryan and Keith Dakin came to accompany me to walk the almost 60 kilometers needed for me to catch up to our caravan and arrive at our latest basecamp, which was moved to the ruins of al-Monqora about 30 kilometers from the outskirts of Damascus. Later in the day a van transported Nancy there as well, so she was there to greet me when we finally dragged in just after dark. A bonfire was built up on the hill where our campsite was situated to help us find our way up the hill in the dark.

Wednesday, November 29th. After another long day of walking, we manage to arrive at our new campsite a few miles outside Damascus, near some cone shaped houses about 5 kilometers south of Dumair. Our camels and support crew will camp out here with Souhel Daas, while our team of Pilgrims will spend a few days in the city visiting churches and community leaders. We travel in the vans to the Cham Palace Hotel in Damascus. After showers, and double cheese burgers all the way around for most of the Caravan crew, we all attend a meeting held in our honor at the Melkite Greek Catholic Church, at the Cathedral of Our Lady of the Dormition in Damascus. They trace their history to the early Christians of Antioch of the 1st century A.D., where Christianity was first introduced there by the Apostle Peter.

Positioned on an elaborate stage, the Church's Choir of Happiness (Jaouket Al Farah), made up of 15 men and 21 women, as well as a lute player, keyboardist, and tambourine percussionist, begin the service with a few Arabic hymns.

The Choir of Happiness

Following the music, Peter Thiep delivers a speech to the congregation in Arabic. Unfortunately, Peter's version of Arabic, being rooted in a Sudanese dialect, is sometimes incomprehensive to the crowd, so Nuhad Tomeh translates it into Syrian Arabic. The crowd finds humor in the language differences, laughed at all his jokes, and greeted him with a thunder of applause as he left the stage.

Peter Thiep, With Nuhad Tomeh Translating

Phil Elkins concluded the evening festivities with a rousing speech about how the history of Syrian Christianity has been a beacon of faith for Christian leaders around the world. His closing remarks are met with loud applause by the congregation, as well. However, I think the highlight of the evening for many of our Caravan crew were the beautiful ladies in the choir! Afterward, they invite a number of them to come back to the Cham Palace Hotel for coffee.

Thursday, November 30th. Our devotions today begin with the 75th of the 99 beautiful names of God: AZ-ZAHIR, "The One Who Appears."

In keeping with this promise of God's actions, something totally unexpected and utterly amazing happens to Peter Thiep today. Some of the Pilgrims had some time off from our scheduled events today, and were wandering around the street markets (souks) here in Damascus. Peter was standing on one side of a large tray with various vegetables and wares, when he noticed a person his age standing on the opposite side of the tray. This person had a distinctive scar on his forehead indicating that he was a member of Peter's own Nuer tribe in South Sudan! They talked together for a few minutes, and learned that they had gone to primary school together in the same village many years ago. What are the chances of that!

Peter Thiep's people within the larger Nuer tribe are Catholic Christians from South Sudan, many of whom were forced to flee when the Islamic Arab government in North Sudan tried to force them to join the military and fight their own people. If they had done so, they were promised special financial and educational opportunities. However, rather than fight their own people, many of the Nuer fled to Jordan, Lebanon and Syria. So a number of Nuer men, women, and children were here in Damascus. They had heard on Syrian television about our Pilgrimage, and were hoping for the chance to see us when we were in the city, but they had no idea that one of their own tribe members was among our group. Peter excitedly told us later in the day about his discovery of his own people being here in Damascus, and we began to make plans on getting together with all of them before we leave Damascus.

The staff at the Middle East Council of Churches has arranged for us today and tomorrow to meet with several churches in the area representing various traditions. Today we all meet with his Holiness Patriarch Zakka, of the Syriac Orthodox Church of Antioch and All The East, at the Cathedral of Saint George. According to their Church tradition, they were on of the first Church communities established by the Apostle Paul. We are led into a grand meeting room, and all sit down in a square formation around the Patriarch's stylish golden throne-like chair—an obvious symbol of his rank and importance in the Church. The Patriarch is wearing flowing black robes with a red lining, and is clutching a thin black staff with a silver handle. His own picture is mounted in a giant silver frame and sits proudly above his chair. Next to it, on one side, is a picture of the new President of Syria, Bashar al-Assad, and on the other sides a picture of both of them together (Bashar al-Assad became President on July 17, 2000, following the death of his father, Hafez al-Assad on June 10, 2000).

Once again we were overwhelmed with the graciousness of local hospitality. We were all served tea, then cakes and cookies, then coffee, and then small candies wrapped in attractive plastic wrappers—all brought to us by two bearded men attired in long black robes and head-coverings. I present the Patriarch with a copy of David Bentley's book, **The 99 Beautiful Names of God, For All the People of the Book,** and express our gratitude for the opportunity to share a visit.

Robin Presenting Patriarch Zakka
With One Of Our Books About God's 99 Names

Our next appointment was Sheikh Ahmad Kaftaro, the Muslim Grand Mufti of the Syrian Republic. A Grand Mufti is the leading Mufti of a country. A Mufti is an Islamic jurist qualified to issue a nonbinding opinion (fatwa) on a point of Islamic law (sharia). Sheikh Kaftaro was first elected Grand Mufti for Syria in 1964, and then in 1984 was named to be "Grand Mufti for life". During his many years of influence, he has established some remarkable organizations dedicated to such things as women's education and inter-religious dialogue. We await his arrival in an immaculately white room on the second floor. There is a framed poster-size photograph of a million worshippers gathered at Mecca.

The Grand Mufti, an older man of 85 years, walks in slowly with the aid of his assistant and a cane. But upon being seated he instantly becomes reinvigorated, declaring, "I welcome all those who love our Father Abraham!" He then briefly explains to us the beliefs of Islam concerning the basic moral framework of our lives while on earth. I then present the Grand Mufti with a copy of David Bentley's book, and briefly describe the purpose of our Pilgrimage—to honor Jesus, the Prince of Peace, on the 2000th year of His birth by having a **"Pilgrimage for Peace"**, and attempting to retrace the original route of the Magi.

Presenting David Bentley's Book
to the Grand Mufti

Later in the afternoon we visit the gigantic Ommayed Mosque, begun in 706 and completed in 715 A.D. It is one of the largest and oldest Mosques in the world. Some Muslims here believe it to be the place where Jesus will return at the "End of Days". Afterwards we all walk to a nearby church to attend an ecumenical meeting, where representatives from different Christian denominations ask questions about our International Pilgrimage.

Robin, Nancy and Pilgrim Crew
Answering Questions About Our Pilgrimage

Friday, December 1st. Andre Martinez seems to have a stomach virus. We have a doctor come and check him out. The rest of us go sightseeing in Damascus. We visit the small church of Ananias, commemorating the man who restored the sight of Saul (the sworn enemy of Jesus, who is then baptized and becomes the Apostle Paul—see Acts 9, verses 10-19). Then we go to the Damascus wall where they think Paul was lowered in a large basket during the night through an opening in the city wall to escape those who planned to murder him (Acts 9.23-25).

After a day of tourism we meet with three different church groups. We first meet with Rev. Boutros Zahour and the leadership of the Damascus National Presbyterian Church.

Our Pilgrim Team Meeting with Church Leaders
at the National Presbyterian Church in Damascus

After our meeting with the Church leadership, we are lead into the basement, where a large group of children are loudly celebrating Saint Barbara's Day (St. Barbara was the daughter of a king who converted from paganism to Christianity, and was subsequently martyred). Though the purpose of the holiday is to re-enact her story, it is celebrated in a fashion similar to Halloween in America. As the music played, the children screamed and ran chaotically about, dressed as gypsies, bunnies, and Superman, among other costumes.

Our second meeting is at the Greek Orthodox Patriarchate of Antioch and All The East with Bishop Ghattas Hazim.

Group Meeting with Bishop Ghattas Hazim
of the Greek Orthodox Church

Our third meeting is with the Greek Catholic Patriarchate of Jerusalem and Alexandria (which had broken with the Greek Orthodox churches in 1724, aligning with Rome but keeping Greek Orthodox traditions). The Bishop explains his perspective on the purpose of the church. "We work for the union of the churches...the truth in Jesus Christ is to accept all others who call on His name. When you arrive in Bethlehem, open your eyes and see the truth." Strong words, which ring in our ears as we return to the Damascus Cham Palace Hotel for a much needed night's sleep.

Group Meeting with the Archbishop
of the Greek Catholic Patriarchate

Saturday, December 2nd. The 77th name of the 99 beautiful names of God is AL-WALI, The Ruler. As quoted in David Bentley's book on the 99 names (page 77), Muslim writer Al-Ghazali's reflection on this name is as follows: "So there is no ruler over things except God...He is, first of all, the sole planner, secondly the one who implements the plan by realizing it." Today we hope that our arriving in Bethlehem is part of God's plan, and that all our striving to fulfill this plan will be realized on December 25th.

We give everyone the day off today, without any meetings planned, so they can explore Damascus as they wish. This week, thanks to the help of Dr. Riad Jarjour and Nuhad Tomah, we have been visiting numerous churches from many different denominations and church traditions. But one of the questions we are often asked by the believers in each of these churches is the same: "Does anyone know that we are here?" We are hesitant to give them an honest answer, because we don't want to discourage them. They all plead with us to ask their brothers and sisters in America to pray for them.

I am reminded of the Prophet Isaiah's words in Isaiah 58:6-7 concerning the difference between true and false worship: "Is not this the fast that I choose: to loose the bonds of injustice, to undo the thongs of the yoke, to let the oppressed go free, and to break every yoke? Is it not to share your bread with the hungry, and bring the homeless poor into your house; when you see the naked to cover them, **and not to hide yourself from your own kin?** We need to ask ourselves, "Are these believers here in Syria truly our brothers and sisters?"

I believe they are. As it is set forth in First Corinthians, Chapter 12:12-13: "For just as the body is one, and has many members, and all the members of the body, though many, are one body, so it is Christ. For in the one Spirit we were all baptized into one body—Jews or Greeks, slaves or free—and we were all made to drink of one Spirit."

Sunday, December 3rd. Our meditation this morning is on the 78th of the beautiful names of God: AL_MUTAALI, "The Most High." The Lord is over all things, and over all of us. Therefore we are called to live justly, practice mercy, and walk humbly before the Most High.

This morning Peter Ryan, our Palestinian camera man Ghassan, and our Sudanese refugee Peter Thiep accompany Thomas Bol, one of the Sudanese refugees now living in Damascus, to several Sudanese apartments in one of the Palestinian refugee camps of Damascus. The camps are tightly packed buildings in large ghettos. Entering one of these homes they are greeted by Chuol Simon. Peeking into the next room they can see their newborn baby Badhiel, which in Nuer means "Hope", now being cradled in her mother's arms. The room is fairly bare, with a couch and some plastic chairs with a matching table. A small picture of President Bashar al-Assad is taped to the back of the front door.

Three very young Palestinian neighbors wander in behind them, giggling, and ask them a lot of questions in Arabic. The youngest, Camela, asks Ghassan the name of every piece of equipment he has hauled into the room—his camera, tripod, batteries, etc.—promptly responding to each of his answers with, "it's mine!" (which probably means that she would really love to have something like that herself one day!). The oldest boy refuses a piece of candy offered him—a traditional gift to guests when visiting a newborn baby—because this is the month of Ramadan.

They get back to the hotel just in time to drive over with the rest of us for a soccer game, in which six of our soccer crew are matched against a team from the Syrian military league. We lose the match 8-7. Our excuse is that half the team has been struggling with illnesses, and our entire soccer crew have also been greatly fatigued by many weeks of walking through the desert. Getting back to the hotel, the soccer crew has time for a quick shower before one last interview with a reporter from the Syrian media.

Then we all go down to the Cham Palace Hotel's Chinese restaurant, where we have managed to gather together, thanks to Peter Thiep, nearly 60 South Sudan refugees from around Damascus, including many mothers with babies and small children. Surviving day to day as refugees in Damascus, all are very happy to have a meal where you can have all you can eat! And my wife Nancy is thrilled to go around and greet all the precious babies being held by a number of the women, as well as the many young children sitting beside them. For Nancy, this night stands out as one of the most outstanding events of our journey.

Peter Thiep welcomes them all, and leads everyone in a prayer of thanksgiving for God's blessing in allowing us to find one another. Then Peter explains his spiritual purpose in attempting the journey by reading to them the passage in Isaiah 18:7. By bringing a gift to honor Jesus, the Prince of Peace, on His 2000th birthday, in that place where salvation came down, Peter is hoping to fulfill this prophecy and thereby bring peace to his people in South Sudan.

Peter's hopeful purpose is fitting on this particular day, which happens to be the first Sunday of Advent. The first candle on the traditional Advent wreath represents the spirit of hope, as we anticipate Christ's coming. Indeed, we Christians are to be in the world as the eyes of hope, always looking for the movement of God's Spirit in new ways and new places. And I believe that's exactly why we find ourselves here, at this time and in this place.

During our meal together, we invite any of the Sudanese men who wish to do so to walk with us for the next 5 days to the Jordanian border. Seven men gladly volunteer to share this experience with us. Others very much wished they could, but their jobs would not allow them to leave Damascus, and they are deeply disappointed. A number of teenage boys are also extremely eager to join us, but their commitments to school would not allow them to take part either (and they of course are equally disappointed).

Over the past five days in Damascus, we have met with five different branches of the ancient Eastern churches, as well as with the Evangelical Presbyterians, Baptists, and of course, the Catholics of Peter Thiep's Nuer tribe. It has been our desire at the outset, by our words and actions, to live out the admonition of the Apostle Paul in the Book of Ephesians, Chapter 4, verses 3-5: "…making every effort to maintain the unity of the Spirit in the bond of peace. For there is one body and one Spirit, just as you were called to the one hope of your calling, one Lord, one faith, one baptism, one God and Father of all, who is above all and through all and in all."

Monday, December 4th. We leave the Cham Palace Hotel in Damascus without Andre Martinez or Jason Drake, both fighting off some stomach bug (a common occurrence for visitors in the Middle East). As we depart, our seven new Sudanese friends join us. One of them, Joshua Daniel, is about 6'8" tall. He did not have any adequate shoes to hike with, so I was able to provide him with my size 14 tennis shoes. A perfect fit!

Seven Nuer Men Join Our Pilgrimage

From the back of one of our camels we wave our brand new **Journey of the Magi** flag, white with gold letters in English, and on the flipside, in Arabic. Our new Sudanese Pilgrims, all tall enough to be professional basket ball players, make our Caravan an even more entertaining spectacle. We are followed by large crowds of children for most of the day. Some of them want to practice their English with us. "Good morning!", one of them shouts. "What is your name? How are you?" Todd Elkins starts handing out candy, word of which quickly spreads throughout our accompanying parade of children, making Todd's generosity in high demand.

Our Sudanese Pilgrims are able to chatter with the children in Arabic. One of them, Tito, to entertain the children, hops on to a camel, and gets some laughs from the children and some of our Caravan crew— his legs are so long that even though sitting up on the camel, his feet are almost touching the ground. We do 37 kilometers for the day, and then are taken forward to our new basecamp. After breaking the Ramadan fast with a cookie, those who fasted today are eager to join us all for dinner around the fire in the Bedouin tent. Nancy stays back in Damascus with our sick Media crew. I crawl into my sleeping bag and fall asleep in minutes—maybe less.

Tuesday, December 5th. As Peter Ryan remarked in his diary, "The only equivalent I can think of to a large group of foreigners passing through a Middle Eastern village on camelback, is the arrival of a circus caravan through the streets of a major city." Today a man on a four-wheel scooter (three in back and one tire up front) drove along side our Caravan for about half a kilometer, holding a young child to his chest, pointing at us and yelling enthusiastically. Another young boy burst into tears at the mere sight of one of our camels.

Syrian media continue to follow us and seek interviews concerning our Pilgrimage for Peace. Todd Elkins does his best to keep them updated about our determination to arrive in Bethlehem on Christmas Day, despite all the reports of continuing violence in Bethlehem.

Todd Elkins Speaking to the Syrian Media

During the day, some of the members of our caravan had been "camel surfing"—standing on top of the saddle as the camel walked through town. So at lunch, we watched in absolute amazement as Bazio, one of our Syrian companions from Souhel's **Bel Tours** crew, completed a back flip from the top of a camel. The media crew had him do it twice, so they could get it on film. Bazio clearly won today's award for acrobatics. Later in the day a large group of young boys on bicycles began riding circles around our caravan. Joshua Daniel, the tallest of our Sudanese Pilgrims, hopped onto one of their bikes—a bike which was barely tall enough to reach his knees. He teetered around on it like a clown on a unicycle. Several other Pilgrims followed his example, and climbed onto the backs of some of the children's bikes as they continued to circle around the Caravan. It's been a fun day.

Wednesday, December 6th. We began the day with a meditation on the 81st of the 99 beautiful names of God: AL-MUNTAQIM, The Avenger. The Apostle Paul, following in the steps of the risen Lord and Messiah, gives instructions to us in Romans Chapter 12:21 concerning not repaying evil for evil. "Do not be overcome by evil, but overcome evil with good."

As part of our morning devotions, we prayed for peace within Sudan and within Palestine, because as I explained, "Both situations are equally discouraging. Each has lasted more than 50 years, with no end in sight. I don't know of any man-made effort that can solve these conflicts. All we can do is pray." So we prayed. Prosper Kwenda from Zimbabwe, a country also experiencing much turmoil and economic hardship, prayed for "an invasion of righteousness" for Israel, Palestine, Sudan, and his own country, Zimbabwe.

Phil Elkins receives word this morning from Sami Awad in Bethlehem that shelling from Israeli tanks and large guns has continued throughout the city. Several windows have been shattered at the Bethlehem Bible College, where a number of us were staying just a few months ago. Despite the continued violence, and the fears of us and many others about the possible "cancellation of Christmas" in Manger Square this year, Sami assures us that he is making arrangements for us to gain entrance into Israel and Bethlehem, and once again urges us to "keep on coming! Our Pilgrimage has been on the radio and TV news in Palestine and many are looking forward to our arrival!"

Phil also learns from Sami some further bad news. The group that Daoud Kuttab had arranged for us to manage our Caravan in Jordan had decided to double the price. Right away, Phil asked Souhel Daas, "Is there any way that you could arrange to provide our support in Jordan?" If so, then Phil would ask Sami to tell Daoud to cancel our prior arrangements. Souhel responded, "Yes! I will handle it! We are one with you in this journey. This is our Pilgrimage too, now!".

Walking in the afternoon, I come across an older gentleman who is part of the Druze community. The Druze are a religious movement that started under the Fatimid dynasty in Egypt in the 11th century. They do not follow the Five Pillars of Islam. They number over 500,000 in Syria.

Robin Greeting An Older Member
of the Druze Community

At the end of the day, some of our Caravan crew trudged across a dirt field and crawled beneath a fence to enter a local soccer field. There our Journey of the Magi soccer crew played against a large group of local boys. We lost 3 to 2, much to the delight of the children, who screamed in victory after every goal until they were out of breath. Their reward was several new soccer balls.

Thursday, December 7th. During our morning devotions Jake Martinez recommends that we have a communion service tonight at the Cham Palace Hotel in Bosra, where everyone will be staying. This would be a good way to honor, and say goodbye, to our Sudanese fellow Pilgrims.

Back out on the road south, we travel through Sweda, where we visit a Catholic church and talk with the Priest, who tells us proudly that they have just completed a Youth Hostel to receive Syrian visitors and other tourists. Toward the end of the day we all stop at a local restaurant. But Jake and Andre Martinez, who were fasting, travel on ahead with Souhel Daas to the Cham Palace Hotel in Bosra. Later that night they join us all for dinner by ordering a grilled half-chicken, in keeping with the Ramadan tradition of generous dinners following a day of fasting.

Tonight we all gather on the top floor of the Bosra Cham Palace to hold the communion service suggested by Jake this morning. Our Sudanese Pilgrims begin to sing songs of worship in the language of their birth, but we are shortly interrupted by the arrival of another Syrian media crew, making a lot of noise setting up a giant flood light and other equipment, and thus killing for the moment our desire for a quiet, worshipful atmosphere. As Peter Ryan would later that evening mention in his journal, "Our communion had, it seemed to me at the time, been degraded to the status of a 'photo opt'. I should have felt grateful to the local press for spending so much time and energy to capture the spirit of our journey, but all I could think about at the moment was how absurd it all seemed." He no doubt gave expression to what a number of us perhaps felt about the interruption at that moment.

Just when we are settling back into a quiet, worshipful atmosphere, to further confuse things, a group of about fifteen middle age tourists from Catalonia clatter up the stairs to join us. They perhaps thought we were having a party, and thought it would be interesting to join in. Only a couple of the Catalonians speak English, but we do our best to explain to them the purpose of our Pilgrimage, honoring Jesus on His 2000th birthday. In short, we have gathered here in this upstairs room to celebrate the meaning of Christmas. They in turn explain this to the rest of their group. After a bit of prodding, they decide to stay. While some of our crew may have also experienced the arrival of the Catalonians as an "interruption", my wife Nancy still fondly remembers their coming up to join us as one of the highlights of our Pilgrimage—that the Lord had indeed blessed us with their presence.

We are able to convince them to sing a few Christmas carols in Catalan, their native tongue. They follow this by singing the national anthem of Catalonia! The ones who speak English also explain some of their own Christmas traditions, including that every year in Catalonia the children would excitedly await the arrive of the three wise men, who would bring presents to people's homes (like our Santa Claus tradition of presents in our homes at Christmas). Then we and the Sudanese sing a few more Carols and hymns, and Andre Martinez plays his guitar and sings the song he wrote during our first week in Syria—**Deeper**—drawing the largest applause of the night. Following this, our Catalonian quests warmly thank us for allowing them to join us, and depart down the stairs. Following their departure, we begin our communion service. Phil Elkins reads some scripture, and passes the bread and wine, and I close the evening with prayer at about 11:30 p.m. It has been a long day.

Friday, December 8th. Some of our crew take the day off to explore Bosra. Meanwhile, I have a van take me back to where we ended the day last night, and walk from there to the border. On the other side of the border from Bosra are the ruins of Umm el-Jimal (which means

"Mother of Camels"). At the beginning of the 1st century, the Nabataean trade route pasted through these two outposts. The Nabataeans were a tribe whose principal capital was located at Petra in southern Jordan. They became quite wealthy from their control of trade routes coming out of Egypt and Arabia and heading north into Europe, and east into Asia. Once we are in Jordan I will circle back to Umm el-Jimal and start walking from the Syrian border there (trying to stay as close as possible to the existing caravan route at the time of the original Journey of the Magi).

Saturday, December 9th. Today, despite the rain this morning, we say goodbye to our Syrian camels and camel drivers, and to some of our support crew working for Souhel, who have to go back to Palmyra. They have done a great job putting up with us! We also say goodbye to our Sudanese fellow Pilgrims. We pray for them and see them off in vans to take them back to Damascus. They have lifted the spirits of our weary ban of Pilgrims, and have been a special blessing to Peter Thiep and all the rest of our Pilgrim crew.

CHAPTER FOUR

✦ ———————— ✦

CARAVANING IN JORDAN

Souhel Daas will be running our basecamp while we are in Jordan, and he has managed to arrange for some of his support crew to come over into Jordan with us. Daoud Kuttab, who is coordinating the work of **The Journey of the Magi 2000: A Pilgrimage for Peace** in Jordan, meets us at the official board crossing on the Jordanian side of the border, along with his daughter, Tamara, and his mother, Maha. Tomorrow Tamara and her grandmother will be walking with us. Our basecamp is now right outside our hotel—the Olive Branch Hotel in Jerash. Jason Drake is very sick from a stomach virus. John Vencer may have the same thing. Good thing we are in a hotel, or more might be getting sick from the cold rain. Again, we prayed for rain—and we got it! Lots of it.

Sunday, December 10th. Today is the second Sunday of Advent for churches around the world. Advent is a time to remember the outpouring of God's love in the past on our behalf. By remembering all the ways in which God has been faithful to us, we renew our courage and vision for living faithfully today in the face of present difficulties and an unknown future.

Today we split up into two groups. Part of the Caravan crew goes with me back to the border at Umm el-Jimal. Somehow, I convince a border security guard to let me step across the border to allow me to follow

150

my own footprints from Syria into Jordan. Shortly after getting under way, about 10:30 in the morning, a newsman from Jordanian TV stops us in order to conduct an interview with me and the other members of the crew. We walk a few yards over to a Bedouin tent, where we are welcomed very graciously. Due to Ramadan, however, no tea or coffee is offered. More cameramen, more filming, more interviews. As Peter Ryan would later remark in his diary that evening, "Sometimes the 'walking' aspect of our Pilgrimage is low on the list of priorities." We don't get underway again until about noon. We still have many miles to cover, if we are to reach Bethlehem by Christmas.

When we stop for lunch, some of our soccer players pass the ball around with some of the children who have gathered around us. We walk for a few more hours and then go back to the hotel—because our soccer players have a game planned that is to be played on real turf against a local team. Tamara Kuttab and her grandmother Maha walked with us today—Maha has arranged for her local church in Amman, Jordan to make contributions to a local charity based on how many miles she walks.

Later, for dinner, some of the caravan crew go out to a nearby Kentucky Fried Chicken (!), where they see a local news story about our Pilgrimage on TV. But due to the ongoing violence, some local newspapers are still predicting the **cancelation** of Christmas festivities in Manger Square in Bethlehem on Christmas Day. Really???

Monday, December 11th. A doctor has now indicated that Jason Drake's illness is a bad case of "Giardia". This is not good—could take awhile to get over it. This is what happens when accepting a sip of water whenever offered by locals. Hospitality here is sometimes hard to refuse, because we are trying so hard to respect their culture and the customs.

Following our day's hike, which is uneventful, we return in the evening for a special event in our Bedouin tent behind our hotel. We are joined in the tent tonight by Mr. Kheirey, the owner of the Olive Branch Hotel, and his family. Originally from Jordan, they had lived in Austin, Texas for many years before moving back to Jerash so that their two daughters could maintain some of their Arab language and culture. Tomorrow his two daughters will walk with us—the younger daughter Deema will skip school from an American high school in Amman to join us. The older daughter Seema was pulled out of a college in Palestine about a month after the recent conflicts began there, so she is looking forward to having something exciting to do.

After a good dinner in the tent, there are bagpipers and drums there to entertain us, and soon they are playing traditional Middle Eastern songs. Most of the people in the room are able to sing along with the songs, and we try to clap along with the beat, but the whine of the bagpipes drowns out the sound of our hands. Soon after that many are up dancing to the beat of the music, and pulling many of us up to join them. The evening is very entertaining, and we leave the tent to go back to our hotel rooms in high spirits.

Keith Dakin and Tim McClelland
Enjoying a Good Dinner at the Olive Branch Hotel Party

Jordanian Bagpipers

Tuesday, December 12th. Our meditation this morning is on the 87th of the 99 beautiful names of God: AL-JAME, "The Gatherer". As is made plain in Isaiah 56:8, "Thus says the Lord God, who gathers the outcasts of Israel, I will gather others to them besides those already gathered." This is a caution to all Christians to be humble and gracious to all, including the outcast and the stranger we may encounter on the way.

We are hardly under way, when Keith and Jake come across the sound of a whimpering puppy, and see one trying to climb up the slope. Two others are further down the slope, shivering and too weak to move. They are female puppies that had been abandoned along the side of road. They are all gathered up by our Caravan crew—no doubt rescuing them from certain death. I try to caution the rescuers that the words "dirty dog" is like a swear word in Arab cultures, and maybe dogs aren't appreciated in Arab culture in the same way that they might be in our own. But they ignore me (thankfully for the puppies sake), clean and feed them, and move them into one of our vans. They have already given them names!

As Peter Ryan later comments in his diary, "the metaphorical significance of rescuing these puppies, which gave life to today's name for God— **Al-Jame'**, the Gatherer—was as irresistible as their timid whines for help." Nancy is very excited to see the puppies at the conclusion of our day. In the days going forward, she and Keith will go around collecting scraps of meat from all of us at meal time to make sure the puppies get their strength back.

Souhel Daas Collecting Rescued Puppies in a Box

The Puppies Being Shown Off
On Top of Our Journey Flag

We end today's walk approaching the ruins of Jerash, which date back to the Roman era, with a very impressive Amphitheatre, and an equally impressive arrangement of intricately carved stone pillars. Before coming down the hill to the Amphitheatre, we have our four Magi change into their costumes, and arrange our display of international flags on the sides of our camels. Seema wears one of the "Queen" outfits which we have had, but have only now had the opportunity to use. As Jake would later write in his diary, "she was stunning!" She quickly became the main target of the cameramen, from French newspapers, to Jordanian TV, to our own media crew.

Our Pilgrim Crew Coming into Jerash

We are met on the large stage by the Mayor of Jerash, and there with the Mayor is our by now good friend, His Excellency Akel Biltaji, the Jordanian Minister of Tourism and Antiquities, all the way up from Amman. We are honored that he has come here to welcome us. After about an hour of posing for photographs, Peter Ryan asks Seema what she thinks of being a tourist attraction. "Actually", she replies, "I don't think I like it all that much".

Nancy Receiving a Rose
From the Mayor of Jerash

Our Magi at the Jerash Amphitheater

Back at the Olive Branch Hotel that evening, everyone watches the T.V. for the evening news in hopes that another story about our trip would appear, as it has for the past few days. We are not disappointed.

Wednesday, December 13th. The 88th of the beautiful names of God is AL-GHANI, "The One Who Enriches." As it says in Psalm 65:9, "You visit the earth and water it, you greatly enrich it."

Today, the Lord has again answered our many prayers for rain with an abundance of it. In the morning we struggle (grumbling) through the rain and mud, but this is exactly what we asked for, right? Today we are attempting to cross up and over the Gilead mountains. The fog gets thicker and the stiff wind gets stronger as we climb further and further up the side of the mountain. At some point Tamara, Maha, Seema and Peter Ryan, discouraged by the elements, crawl back into the van and turn back to the hotel. As the day goes on up here on the mountain, it doesn't get any better. Soon the sleet turns to hail, and then to snow! Who ever would have expected such a thing?

The snow clings to my eyelashes as I keep moving on up, walking into the face of the storm. Actually, I am loving it! Reminds me of a few of my late summer experiences in California's Sierra Nevada mountains, where we got unexpected snow—but that was at 11,000 feet elevation! I don't think we will be at any more than 3000 feet elevation here.

Some of our crew miss out on this excitement, as they go on a side trip up to the ruins of a church that marks the place where the prophet Elijah went to hide from Jezebel (I Kings 19:8-9). Most of the media crew go with them, so I am not sure we have captured the snowstorm for posterity. Upon returning to our basecamp, everyone gathers in our Bedouin tent on the grounds of the Olive Branch Hotel to enjoy a Mansaf feast to mark the end of fasting for the day.

Except for me—when I get back I am exhausted and go to bed. Then our Caravan crew drive to the Baptist Church of Jerash, where some of the congregation have gathered in their small building to greet us. The following is a record of the evening as described in Peter Ryan's journey.

Pastor Issac welcomes us, and then Todd Elkins makes a brief speech about our Journey, with young Tamara Kuttab translating. The small children's choir—made up of young girls—sing a Christmas song in Arabic to the tune of "Old Susanna". Then, while the children sing a few more Arabic Christmas carols, a meal is served to us by our hosts. We respond in turn by singing "Silent Night" in English, after which they need to sing for us the **real** version—in Arabic! Following this, the children sing more Christmas carols in Arabic, with us joining in English, creating a somewhat chaotic harmony.

Then things get even sillier. The children sing several songs involving increasingly rapid movements of the hands, almost always ending with a series of mistakes by us, with the girls erupting into giggles. Ending the evening, we sing "Father Abraham", which after every chorus adds on a new activity for the hands and feet, eventually becoming too complex for the body to manage—especially for us! We leave the church in good spirits, and with a few new friends (and maybe a few new songs!).

Thursday, December 14th. On our walk this morning we come down off the mountain and enter the Jordan valley. As Peter Ryan would comment later that evening in his journal, "The terrain is absolutely spectacular: large white boulders, beautiful brown horses, mossy green hills—the kind of landscape I'd expect to see in Ireland, not in a desert of the Middle East." We can already begin to see the mountains of the Palestinian territories off in the distance. As we get closer and closer to our ultimate destination, the media coverage is increasing. While we have yet to see it ourselves, it has been confirmed that our International Pilgrimage has made it onto the headlines of CNN International!

We end our walk today at the Mosque (and tomb) of the Venerable Companion to Mohammed, Abu Ubeida ibn Al-Jarrah. He was a relative of the Prophet, and one of the first converts to Islam. He was one of the "Blessed Ten" to whom the Prophet promised paradise. He served as the Supreme Commander of the Northern Muslim Army, and was named by Mohammed as the "Trustee of the Nation". Today the Mosque serves as a major Islamic center, and non-Muslims are not allowed entrance into the Mosque itself.

After a guard in a military jumpsuit politely explains this to me and the rest of our entourage, I walk as far as he allows me to, then take off my shoes, customary for entering a Mosque, and open up my arms out wide with uplifted hands in prayer. I silently stand there for about five minutes, until the guard finally relents and allows the whole group to enter the main temple (with shoes off). Maybe it was my praying—maybe it was that I have a flowing long white beard—maybe both. In any case, we might be among the first non-Muslims to ever enter the building.

After visiting the Mosque, our next stop is the Union Alliance Church of Mafraq, where a graduation service is being held for some younger members of the congregation entering into the Youth Group division of Sunday School. After several hymns are sung, accompanied by an Arabic **Oud** (lute), Todd Elkins speaks a few words about the purpose of our Pilgrimage, and Peter Thiep ceremoniously presents the graduates with gifts.

When we arrive back to the Olive Branch Hotel for the night, the Kheirey family has arranged a special dessert send off to say goodbye, with tea and **Qataif,** a rolled up taco-shaped pancake coated with either nuts or cheese, and dipped into a giant bowl of maple syrup. They are an amazing family, and have been the most gracious and generous hosts! We will miss them all! Tomorrow we will, once again, move our basecamp down the road.

Friday, December 15th. A shorter day today—maybe no more than 15 kilometers. Most of the soccer crew—Tim McClellan, Todd Elkins, Prosper Kwenda, and Keith Dakin—run most of the way.

Today, Souhel Daas walks with me most of the way, including passing through the village of Dhofar. We are so thankful that Souhel has been able to continue providing support for us in Jordan. His helpful translation and encouragement at times like this is invaluable.

Souhel Daas and Robin
Walking Through the Village of Dhofar

Robin Shaking Hands With Local Youth

At the conclusion of our hike, we drive to our new basecamp. Our new campsite is near the location of recent archaeological excavations that have validated the fact that this is where Jesus was baptized by John the Baptist, on the east side of the Jordan River, just above the Dead Sea (see the Gospel of John, Chapter 1:28-34).

Saturday, December 16th. We had kind of a short day yesterday. Today we are going to have to make up for it, and go all the way from where we ended yesterday to our basecamp at the Baptismal site of Jesus. After about 15 kilometers we stop and rest in the shade of some nearby trees. I have to wait for a phone call interview, to be broadcast live on Bethlehem 2000 Radio. Our three white puppies, meanwhile, entertain us by frolicking around in the dirt.

Gradually, most of the caravan crew pull themselves up on their feet and continue on down the road. I stay behind waiting for my call. Eventually, the call does come and I answer several questions, always mentioning the overwhelming generosity and kindness of the people we have met all along the way—in Iraq, in Syria, and now here in Jordan. Then I hand the phone over to Tamara and Peter Thiep for their interviews in Arabic. Back on the road once again, I am now bringing up the rear, and I try my best to make up ground the rest of the day.

At the end of today's 40 kilometers hike, we gather in the Ministry of Tourism building near the Baptismal site and dig into a generous meal of Mansaf. During the meal we enjoy a Tourism video about Jordan, and a slide show about the excavation going on at the Baptismal site. Then I sneak off with Nancy to the Movenpic Hotel nearby to collapse.

But our tireless crew of Pilgrims change into their Magi costumes and drive off 30 minutes up the hill to Amman's Holiday Inn, where local Christians have gathered for a Christmas celebration. Over 200 people in the dining room are shown a short video of our journey, which receives a warm round of applause. Then each member of the team is briefly introduced. A buffet dinner follows, and then a local preacher gives a sermon about the journey of the original Wise Men—"men who were searching for the truth." At the conclusion of the evening a gift raffle is held which seems oddly stacked in our favor. Peter Ryan, Prosper, Souhel, Jason Drake, and one of the van drivers all receive prizes. They don't arrive back at our campsite until nearly midnight, some too tired to even pull off their costumes. They just crawl into bed.

Sunday, December 17th. We began the morning with a meditation on the 92nd of the 99 beautiful names of God: AN-NAFI, "The One Who Grants Favor". Today is the third Sunday of Advent. We are reminded to face tomorrow with joy, and with hope-filled anticipation, because the future belongs to God, who has favored us with His Spirit, and He has promised to go with us into the future as we approach His coming.

On our last day in Jordan, thanks to the arrangements made for us by Jordan's Minister of Tourism and Antiquities, Akel Biltaji, we are given a tour of the area by Dr. Mohammed Waheeb, the archaeologist who rediscovered the authentic Baptismal site of Jesus. The site had been buried for centuries with many layers of sand. Also, large stretches of land on both sides of the Jordan River had been heavily land mined as part of the battles taking place during the Six Day war in 1967. For years thereafter, the whole area was abandoned. Thankfully, de-mining took place following the 1994 Israel-Jordan peace treaty, negotiated by President Bill Clinton with King Hussein of Jordan and Prime Minister Yitzhak Rabin of Israel.

Following the de-mining, as Dr. Waheeb tells the story, God told him to begin excavating here, because "this was the actual place where Jesus was baptized". He subsequently was able to uncover the remains of an ancient monastery built on the hill where Elijah was "taken up to heaven in a chariot of fire", as well as the remains of several more monasteries, built over several centuries, marking the spot where, indeed, Jesus was baptized by John the Baptist. Explaining all this to us, Dr. Waheeb quotes a number of pages from the New Testament by memory, using the witness of Scripture as to the authenticity of the site.

As we finish our visit at the Baptism of Jesus, we are able to present Dr. Waheeb with one of our Journey of the Magi flags, to thank him for all the time he has spent with us today, and especially for his willingness to trust in God's urging him to dig in this place. Thankfully, in 2015 UNESCO designated Jesus' Baptismal site as a World Heritage site.

Presenting Dr. Waheeb with One
of Our Journey of the Magi Flags

Inspired by Dr. Waheeb's testimony, several of our Caravan crew, including Peter Thiep, choose to be baptized here where Jesus was baptized.

Being our last day in Jordan, we also have many heartfelt thanks to express to all those who have helped us so much over the past several weeks. Following Jesus' own example, when he washes the feet of his disciples, we Pilgrims ceremoniously wash the feet of all of our support crew—including the van drivers, our camel guides, our Jordanian guide, and of course, the amazing Souhel Daas.

Robin, Nancy and Phil Elkins
Explaining Jesus' Example of Foot Washing

Pilgrim Crew Washing the Feet
of Those Who Have Served Us

After dinner we set up a huge semi-circle of plastic chairs extending from our Bedouin tent "dining" area, which has now been converted into a makeshift stage. A choir made up of perhaps a dozen Sudanese singers who may have heard about us from the Sudanese refugees in Syria, have come down from Amman to join us, and they perform for us two songs in Arab. A number of Jordanians from local churches in Amman have also come to take part in the Christmas service, and a large choir of perhaps 40 people perform several Christmas carols in English.

Choir Singing Christmas Carols in English

By this time, I am not feeling well, and creep off to bed at the Movenpik Hotel close by. So when the choir is finished, Phil Elkins introduces the Caravan crew for me, and explains to the growing crowd one of the purposes of our journey—to honor Jesus by promoting peace among all people, Christian and Muslim, throughout the region.

Then John Vencer follows Phil with an announcement: "About five days ago, we found three puppies on the side of the road. We've grown quite attached to the little mongrels. But since we can't take them with us across the border tomorrow, we were wondering if any of the families here would be willing to adopt them?" Almost before he could finish his sentence, a number of hands shot up. So Keith Dakin and my wife Nancy, who were perhaps among the most attached to the puppies, organized a lottery by putting the names of the interested families into a jar. Three families go home very happy, but a few others are equally disappointed. But at least the puppies now have good homes.

Winning A Puppy

In the middle of all this, our soccer crew departs to play a soccer match under the lights in Amman. Following the match, Jake and Andre Martinez go to pick up their mom, Gail Martinez, and their younger brother Jason from the airport, who have arrived from the U.S. to share in the final chapter of our journey. My son Mark has also been able to join us for the final push, God willing, up to Bethlehem.

CHAPTER FIVE

❖

CARAVANING UP TO BETHLEHEM

onday, December 18th. At about 3 a.m. I become extremely ill, and can't hold anything down. This goes on for the rest of the night (poor Nancy!). Some who later hear about it suspect I have Giardia, like Jason Drake had come down with the previous week, but I am hoping it is a temporary case of food poisoning. In any case, when our Caravan of Pilgrims depart early this morning, I am not able to join them. Joined by our newly arrived Pilgrims, including my son Mark Wainwright, and Gail Martinez and her son Jason, everyone begins walking from our basecamp near the Baptismal site to the Israel-Jordan border, saying goodbye to all our friends along the way.

Praying At The Jordanian Border

Surprisingly, Sami Awad has been able to make arrangements for the entire Pilgrim caravan to **walk** across the entire no-mans land between the borders, which is extensively guarded by machine gun turrets, land mines, and barbed wire—perhaps the first such exception known in recent memory. Everything went well until half way across, when there were reports of violence in Jericho, and they were stopped and asked to get on an Israeli bus for the rest of the crossing. The first bus soon got a flat tire, and they had to wait for another bus. Then they had to unload all their equipment off the first bus and on to the new one. At this point, Todd Elkins and Keith Dakin decide to go back to Jordan. They had been hoping to either walk or ride camels the entire way, in keeping with the original Magi. Now they would try to do so again tomorrow.

Unfortunately, upon arriving at the passport office at the Israeli border, three of our Pilgrims were held up because of visa issues—Prosper Kwenda of Zimbabwe, Peter Thiep of Sudan, and John Vencer of the Philippines. The whole Caravan crew waits around as a group for them, while they continue to work on getting the three of our Magi into Israel. The BBC and ABC and other press were outside waiting, but most of them eventually give up and move on. Finally Phil Elkins and Jake and Andre Martinez leave the group and go through to meet the press, but by that time there was only one lady and a couple of photographers still waiting for an interview.

John Vencer is finally allowed to pass through and join the group, and they all arrive at their hotel in Jericho at around 7 p.m. They are met by Dr. Saeb Erekat, the chief Palestinian peace negotiator. They are also met by Sami Musalam, the head government official for Jericho, Ismael Al-Jamal, the local Grand Mufti, the local Palestinian chief of Police, the local head of the Palestinian military, and several other leaders of Christian Churches and ministries. Somewhere in that crowd they are also eventually able to find and greet Sami Awad and Awni Jubran, from the Bethlehem Holy Land Trust office.

Meanwhile, back at our hotel at the Dead Sea, Nancy and I are awakened sometime after 9 p.m. by a knock on the door. Upon opening the door, we find Prosper Kwenda and Peter Thiep, our two black African Magi, standing outside. They have been denied entry into Israel. Thank the Lord we were here for them. What would have happened if I had not gotten sick, and instead of being here to receive them, Nancy and I had gone off this morning with the rest of the Caravan as originally planned? So my being violently ill in the early hours this morning turns out to be a means of grace and hope for our two discouraged Magi. God does work in strange ways sometimes!

Tuesday, December 19th. Todd Elkins and Keith Dakin walk across the border this morning. Though once again granted permission to walk all the way across into Israel, a guard perched up in a gun turret yells at them from a distance, telling them to "come here". Sami Awad, who is accompanying them in his van, yells, "Ignore them. They can only do two things—shout or shoot." They ignore them and keep on walking. Further on, Keith remembers being surprised by several other Israeli soldiers climbing down from their gun position and offering them a cold drink. Eventually, Todd and Keith are able to pass through Israeli customs and meet up with the rest of the Pilgrims in Jericho.

Our Caravan of Pilgrims—hoping that the two Magi who were turned back at the border last night could somehow get into Israel and catch up to them (and me and Nancy with them)—take the day off to tour the city of Jericho and several monasteries nearby. They climb up to the Monastery of Temptation, which was carved directly into the mountainside around 1895. Because of the persistent conflicts going on in the area as a result of the Second Intifada, there are no tourists in the area, and the gondola that usually runs from the middle of Jericho up to the monastery is shut down.

Monastery of Temptation

After visiting several other ruins during the day, our soccer crew was suiting up for a match with the Jericho All-Star team, when four more members of the Charlotte Eagles—Jacob, Donavon, Todd and Nathan—showed up with uniforms for all of them. It rained earlier just enough to make the field a little muddy, and the clay to stick to the bottoms of their soccer cleats, but it was a high energy soccer match, with our soccer crew winning the match 3-1.

Our Soccer Team Playing Jericho All-Star Team

Their day ended with a breaking of the Ramadan fast at the Jericho offices of Yasser Arafat. A good meal was enjoyed by all, except for Chairman Arafat, who for obvious reasons was absent.

Enjoying A Meal in Chairman Arafat's Office Building

Meanwhile, back at our hotel, we immediately got busy that morning trying to find a way to get our two black African Magi into Israel. First, my wife Nancy has our hotel find the phone number of the American embassy in Jerusalem. Nancy is able to get someone on the phone, and after explaining about our "Pilgrimage for Peace" to honor Jesus on his 2000th birthday, Nancy then tells her about our two black Magi being turned back, while everyone else was allowed to enter. Unexpectedly, but fortuitously, the woman on the other end of the line is a black American from the U.S. She is very, **very** upset about this news, and says that she will get on this right away with some other officials in the American embassy, as well as some contacts she had with Israeli immigration officials.

Jonathan Kuttab, who has numerous contacts with senior officials in the Israeli government, including some members of the Israeli Supreme Court, begins making some calls this morning as well, suggesting to them that in light of the approaching special Christmas Day, on the 2000th anniversary of Jesus' birth, the turning back of our two Magi would not look good for Israel. Daoud Kuttab, who has many media contacts in the U.S., having published articles with such major newspapers as the Los Angeles Times and the Washington Post, also begins making some calls to alert various media contacts in the Middle East and the U.S. about the current situation involving our two Magi, and asking them to contact authorities in Israel about the matter.

Nancy and I spend some time in prayer with Prosper and Peter, and learn from Prosper that he had come to Israel with the Charlotte Eagles in December of 1998, when they were scheduled to play soccer against the Palestinian national team in Gaza. It was the first game played in the new stadium built by the E.U. He was turned back at the Israeli passport office that time as well. He returned to Amman, Jordan and tried to get a visa there, but was again rejected, so he just returned home to the U.S. Having been deeply disappointed on that occasion, he was now not very hopeful that he would be able to join us in Bethlehem on Christmas Day. All we can do now is to just wait and see what might develop as a result of all our phone calls.

Wednesday, December 20th. Today our meditation—for us here at our hotel, and for our Caravan crew in Jericho—is the 95th of the 99 beautiful names of God: AL-BADI, "The Purpose Setter". As the Apostle Paul states in Romans 8:28, "We know that all things work together for good for those who love God, who are called according to his purpose." We continue to pray that, God willing, it will be part of God's purpose for Prosper and Peter to join all the rest of us in Bethlehem on Christmas Day.

Our Caravan of Pilgrims leave their hotel in Jericho and start up the steep narrow road that would eventually—in a few days, God willing—bring them to Bethlehem. They had not gotten far before their camels were blocked by a towering mound of sharp rocks, blasted out by Israeli soldiers to block off all traffic in and out of Jericho. Those who were riding camels had to dismount, and scale the boulders on foot with the rest of the Pilgrims.

Rocks Blocking the Road Up to Bethlehem

Fortunately, waiting for them on the other side of the roadblock are another group of camels—the situation having been anticipated by the support crew of Holy Land Trust in Bethlehem. Also waiting for them on the other side are representatives from the Associated Press and NBC, greeting them with red-lighted Beta cameras and fluffy boom-mikes. Following the interviews they continue on up the road.

Back at the Movenpik Hotel, near the Baptismal site on the east side of the Jordan, we receive a surprise visit from a Muslim taxi driver, who a few days earlier had helped deliver Nancy to our basecamp. Somehow he has heard that I was sick, and has come with his son to pray for me. While we barely knew each other, he knows how important it was to me to be able to reach Bethlehem by Christmas Day, and has come to do whatever he could to encourage me. Both my wife and I are very grateful that he would come far out of his way to see if there was anything he could do for me. His prayers and concern for me does help lift my spirits.

Doubly encouraging is the call we get later in the day, indicating that both Prosper Kwenda and Peter Thiep have received the clearance of their visas (!), and would be eligible to cross over into Israel tomorrow morning. Yes! We forward the good news over to our Pilgrims already there, and tell them that in the morning, God willing, we will **all** try to come over and join them. God, the Purpose Setter, is making the way for us—Prosper and Peter will be with us on Christmas Day in Bethlehem!

Thursday, December 21st. We had an early breakfast at the Movenpik Hotel, and Prosper and Peter walked with me down to the Jordanian passport office. We sent Nancy ahead of us in a van. It was our intention to walk across the entire no-mans land of the border. When we started walking, a Jordanian guard told us that what we were doing was not allowed, but we just kept walking. Eventually, he just waved goodbye to us. A few hours later, Todd Elkins, Keith Dakin, and Peter Ryan came down to the Israeli passport office to meet us. Prosper and Peter Thiep are ecstatic to finally be walking into Israel—fulfilling a long hoped for dream for both of them.

Tonight, back at our new basecamp at Nabi Musa, our entire team of Pilgrims are together for the first time inside Israel, and will be on our way up the hill toward Bethlehem in the morning.

Approaching Our Base Camp at Nabi Musa

We celebrate by enjoying the music played by George Rishmawi of Holy Land Trust and a few of his friends, and then playing several large group games. One game, called "Fruit Salad", causes a few bruises and at least one broken chair, and later ends with a "violent" game of musical chairs, won by Holy Land Trust's Awni. The evening quiets down again as the group gathers around for some songs of worship, only to be interrupted by a catfight on the second floor of the Mosque. One cat, fleeing the battle, comes charging down the stairs toward our group, causing a few screams of alarm. Everyone is so concerned about the cat that most fail to notice the slowly tipping mounted light used by our camera guys, which is about to fall straight onto Gail Martinez's head. "The light! The light!", John Vencer shouts, and even though he is sitting further away from the danger zone than anyone else, he manages to rush out into the center of the floor and catch the light stand before Gail is injured. Whew! I think that is enough excitement for one night.

Friday, December 22nd. We are joined today by several new members of our Pilgrimage: Montseraat Cata, originally from Catalonia, who has been living in Bethlehem and working at the Holy Land Trust office; Dr. Don Wagner, a Professor of Middle East Studies at North Park University, and board member of Holy Land Trust-USA, with his son Matt, and his daughter, Anna; David Bentley, the author of **The 99 Beautiful Names of God, for All the People of the Book**; and Mark Khano, the general manager of Guiding Star LTD tours, with his wife, along with a baby child strapped to his back.

A long section of today's trek takes us through an Israeli firing range, where we pass by many tanks with their engines running, and soldiers sitting on top of the hot metal hoods. They stare in disbelief as our Pilgrims pass them by, with our full array of international flags waving on our twelve camels, and with about thirty Pilgrims either riding the camels or walking along side.

Passing Through Israeli Military Zone

Israeli Tank on Trailer

To reach the day's final destination, we have to climb down a steep ridge, and leap over a polluted creek, before climbing back up another steep ridge to arrive at Mar Saba Monastery. Mar Saba is a Greek Orthodox Monastery overlooking the Kidron Valley, at a point half way between the Old City of Jerusalem and the Dead Sea. Founded by Sabbas the Sanctified in 483, it is considered one of the oldest inhabited Monasteries in the world, and still maintains many of its ancient traditions. The monastery kept its importance even during the existence of the Latin Kingdom of Jerusalem, established by Crusaders in 1099, after the First Crusade. The relics of Saint Sabbas were held there at the monastery, until seized by the Latin Christians in the 12th century, and removed to Italy. In 1965 Pope Paul VI returned Saint Sabbas' relics to the monastery as a gesture of repentance and good will towards Orthodox Christians. The Mar Saba Monastery was also the home of St. John of Damascus (676-749). His tomb lies in a cave underneath the Monastery.

Ancient Monastery of Mar Saba

We were greeted at Mar Saba by Father Lazarus. Years ago he had been a psychology student at the University of California Santa Cruz. While there he began investigating the teaching of the early fathers of the Greek Orthodox Church, and eventually converted to Greek Orthodoxy and came here to live the life of a monk. He explains to our Pilgrims their ancient custom of forbidding women to enter the compound, so the women in our caravan wait patiently (or not!) outside while we go on a short tour through the Monastery.

After departing Mar Saba, we were soon picked up by our vans and taken on to our new basecamp, which had been set up on the basketball court of the Al-Abediah High School for Girls. The facility is guarded by several Palestinian security officers, equipped with old Soviet rifles. After a brief meal, everyone turns in early—definitely in need of some sleep. I have a van take me to Bethlehem Bible College to meet up with Nancy.

Saturday, December 23rd. Our devotion this morning is on the 98th name of God in David Bentley's book: AR-RASHID, "The Right Guide". As set forth in Psalm 25:9, "He leads the humble in what is right, and teaches the humble his way."

Back at our basecamp, we have some time this morning to explore our surroundings at the Al-Abediah High School for Girls. A few unfinished murals on the grounds, with faded black outlines, one showing a young boy with an amputated leg, shouting, "Come on! Is the blindness in your hearts?", and another showing a mother holding a baby in her arms while trapped between rows of barbwire, whispering softly, "They say we have won, my son, why are you crying?"

Our vans finally arrive to drive us to our starting point to begin the day's walk, and we crowd in—because of our growing numbers, many of us sitting on each other's laps or on the floor. We continue working our way up the hill toward Bethlehem. Many children have gathered along the way to see the parade of people and camels passing through their neighborhood.

Working Our Way Up the Hill Toward Bethlehem

Children Watching Our Procession

Later in the morning we climb up a steep hill, and duck under a barbwire fence, before coming upon the outer wall of Saint Theodosios

Monastery. According to tradition, this Monastery was built over the cave that the Wise Men used to hide from King Herod, after greeting the newborn King.

Sami Awad and Jonathan Kuttab join us for the final events of the day. We owe them far more than we can say for all they have made possible for us here in Palestine, and especially in Bethlehem. Without them, our hope for being part of the festivities in Manger Square on Christmas Day would never has come about.

Sami Awad and Jonathan Kuttab

That evening we are taken to Bethlehem's Municipality building, where we break fast with Mitril Abu Ateh, the Ministry of Tourism, and Bishara Daoud, a member of the Palestinian Legislative Council. Mitril Abu Ateh welcomes us with a brief speech: "We hope that you will pass the message back to the people in your countries, and to your governments, that we do not want our children killed, and we do not want the children of others killed. We are people against terrorism, and people against bloodshed. We want to live with freedom, dignity, and independence in a Palestinian nation with a shared Jerusalem, and under the leadership of President Yasser Arafat. We are not here to throw the Jews into the sea, or anything like that. (Someone from the crowd shouts out, "It is they who throw us!", which is answered by a great deal of laughter.) Abu Ateh continues, "It is a blessing that Ramadan and Christmas occur at the same time this year, representing the unity of Christians and Muslims in Palestine."

Then I am asked to respond. "All along the route of our Pilgrimage, literally hundreds of people have asked us: 'Why do you walk? Why are you doing this?'. We never have enough time to give a complete answer. Of course, we are here to honor Jesus on the 2000th anniversary of His birth. But what is it that truly honors Jesus?

It is the pursuit of peace and justice. We are walking for the children of Iraq, who have caught polio from the water poisoned by the U.S. bombing in the Gulf War, because these children will never walk again. We are walking for those here in Palestine whose legs have been shot, who will never walk again. We are walking for the Palestinian children who have died, who will never walk, laugh, or play ever again. We are walking on behalf of everyone, on both sides of this conflict, who by injury or by death, will never walk again. If you believe that Jesus is the Prince of Peace, and that Jesus will judge us all at the Resurrection, as both Christians and Muslims do, then rise up and be warriors for peace. When we reach Bethlehem on Christmas Day, our journey will not have ended. Rather, our journey towards peace and justice will only have just begun. May God bring us peace!"

We end our day with an ecumenical service at the Greek Orthodox Church in Beit-Sahour, where we are warmly welcomed with Christmas songs in Arabic. Then the whole Pilgrim team is brought up on stage to much applause. The evening is concluded with **Oh Little Town of Bethlehem.** Because the song is sung in English on our behalf, we are able to add our voices to the choir. Given the level of violence that has been going on in Bethlehem for the past few months, it seems at the same time to be a form of prayer for the peace that is so badly needed this night.

Girls Choir at the Greek Orthodox Church

We Are All Brought Up On Stage
to Much Applause

Sunday, December 24th. We begin our day with the 99th of the 99 beautiful names of God: AS-SABUR, "The Patient One". Churches around the world are celebrating with us today the fourth Sunday of Advent—holding up for us all the desire for peace among ourselves, and in the world around us. As the Apostle Paul sets forth in Colossians 3:12, "Since God chose you to be the holy people he loves, you must clothe yourselves in tender-hearted mercy, kindness, humility, gentleness, and patience". For the past two months, since departing from Ctesiphon in Iraq, we have tried to live up to this admonition of Saint Paul as we have encountered many different members of the body of Christ, as well as our gracious Muslim hosts, in each country through which our Pilgrimage has taken us.

Returning this morning to where we ended our walk yesterday, we arrive by mid-afternoon in Beit Sahour, where Shepherd's Field is located. Several of us, including Phil Elkins, are interviewed by a local TV station.

Phil Elkins Interviewed By Local TV

Later we attend a Christmas Eve service in a cave where shepherds at one time had kept their flocks—perhaps even on that night long ago when the angel came down to get their attention. As is set forth in the Gospel of Luke, Chapter 2:9-11: "Then an angel of the Lord stood before them, and the glory of the Lord shown around them, and they were terrified. But the angel said to them, 'Do not be afraid, for see—I am bringing you good news of great joy for all the people: to you is born this day in the city of David a Savior, who is the Messiah, the Lord'".

Tonight it is dark and raining, with a fierce wind, but we hurry a few hundred yards off the road to enter the cave. It is quite dark in the cave, but small white pamphlets are passed out to us containing the lyrics of Christmas hymns, and verses about the angel's visit to the shepherds. Eventually, candles are passed around and we are able to sing worshipfully together about our hope—our hope that the Hope of the Ages has indeed come down to this little town in the middle of nowhere, to lift us all up to God.

Robin and Nancy At Christmas Eve Service
In Shepherds Field

Following our Christmas Eve vigil in the cave, we drive back to Bethlehem Bible College for our own Christmas Eve celebration—small and intimate, with no crowds and no reporters for once. We begin the evening with me and Nancy thanking our core Caravan crew, who have carried us day by day all the way from Ctesiphon to Bethlehem. Their skills, stamina, and courage have been extraordinary, especially in light of the fact that there were many days when we were not even sure if there would even be a Christmas in Bethlehem this year, or if we would be able to enter Bethlehem to be part of it. We present each of them with a **Journey of the Magi** flag as a token of our gratitude for their willingness to undertake **The Journey of the Magi 2000: A Pilgrimage for Peace** with us.

After singing a few Christmas carols together, Andre Martinez sings several of the songs he wrote while on our Pilgrimage. To conclude the evening, I read out loud for them the poem by T.S. Eliot, **Journey of the Magi**, written in 1927, imaging the original journey of the three wise men. Some lines in the poem remind us all of things we have experienced together during our own Pilgrimage. Especially these lines:

> *A hard time we had of it...*
> *With the voices singing in our ears, saying*
> *That this was all folly.*

But our journey was not all folly, as it turns out. It was meant to be. If the Lord is in it, all things are possible!

Our Personal Christmas Eve Service
At Bethlehem Bible College

CHAPTER SIX

CHRISTMAS DAY 2000 IN BETHLEHEM

Monday, December 25th. We all gather this morning at Bethlehem Bible College. We begin the day with our devotions meditating on the "100th name of God". We have decided, in keeping with our celebration today of the 2000th anniversary of Jesus's birth, that it should be IMMANUEL, which means, "GOD WITH US!" (See Isaiah 7.14)

One of the many checkpoints surrounding us has blocked our bus from picking us up from Bethlehem Bible College for the events of the day, so we hire taxis to take us to another Israeli checkpoint. At this checkpoint, a Palestinian Christian named Ja'ad shouts to us from his car, "Merry Christmas… This is our Merry Christmas," pointing casually to Israeli soldiers sitting in an armored jeep blocking the road. Ja'ad, with his family packing tightly around him in his car, had just been turned back at an earlier checkpoint on his way to visit relatives on Christmas Day.

Checkpoint in Bethlehem on Christmas Day

At the new checkpoint, we walk about half a kilometer through a drizzling rain, and load into a bus on the other side of the checkpoint. This causes us to be late for our meeting with Faisal Al-Hussani, the Palestinian Mayor of East Jerusalem. Finally reaching the Oriental House in Jerusalem, and pulling off our soaking jackets and hats once inside, we gather around a conference table with Hussani. Welcoming us, the Mayor makes a comment about the checkpoints by telling us a story from his childhood. "I remember once as a child in Egypt watching a film—one of the Tarzan movies. I remember asking my older sister, 'My father is stronger than Tarzan, right?'. Hussani laughs, and continues, "Any child will look to his father in this way. A father is a child's protector, his hero, everything in his life. So what happens when a man is stopped at an Israeli checkpoint, and the soldiers humiliate him, or treat him as though he were nothing, maybe even beating him? To the child, this symbol of power—the father—will collapse. What happens to the child who watches this? Something will have died inside him. He may no longer listen to his father. Deep inside, he will say to himself, 'you can't protect me'. After this sobering insight into the impact of the Israeli checkpoints upon his people, Hussani thanks us for our visit.

We present the Mayor with one of our Journey of the Magi flags. The Mayor shakes hands with Nancy, and extends to us special permission to visit the Al-Aqsa Mosque. We would perhaps be the first tour group to visit the Mosque in almost three months, since the outbreak of the Second Intifada on September 28th.

Presenting Mayor Hussani
With Our Pilgrimage Flag

Nancy Shaking the Mayor's Hand
With Sami Awad Looking On

Our Pilgrims in Front of the Orient House

Our Pilgrims in Front of the Al-Aqsa Mosque

Following our tour of Al-Aqsa, we return to Bethlehem Bible College, where we enjoy a generous Christmas feast. During dinner, Sami Awad informs us of some awesome arrangements that have been made for our four kilometers walk from Shepherd's Field to Manger Square. He has been working closely with Dr. Ghassan Andoni, a Christian from the village of Beit Sahour, and the co-founder of the International Solidary Movement (ISM), for many thousands of Palestinians to gather at Shepherd's Field—Muslims and Christians together—to walk together to Manger's Square. As they approach Manger's Square they will begin carrying torches. They are calling it a **torch parade for peace**, and it will be a spectacular conclusion to our **Pilgrimage for Peace.**

Then everyone gets dressed up in their "Magi" uniforms and heads for Shepherd's Field. It is far beyond anything we could have dreamed of or hoped for. Some later report that as many as 5000 people or more take part in the torch parade. Because of the on-going violence happening over the past few months, the millions of Christians from around the world that had been expected to participate in Bethlehem's celebration of the 2000th anniversary of Jesus' birth are not here. Instead, here we are—our **The Journey of the Magi 2000: A Pilgrimage for Peace**—becoming the main event in Manger Square on Christmas Day for Jesus's 2000th birthday!

As the parade finally gets under way, our caravan of Pilgrims are up in the front, with most of our journeymen riding camels. Nancy rides up in front of them, on the tallest camel of all!

Nancy on the Tallest Camel

As night falls, the torch parade begins. All along the way, people are standing out on their balconies waving to us, some singing Christmas carols. Two of our Pilgrim crew walk out in front of the parade carrying the giant white banner that my wife Nancy has created for the occasion. The banner carries the image of Jesus Christ in tears, wearing a crown of thorns, with the words, "Jesus weeps for Palestinians". Peter Ryan follows with our Journey of the Magi banner.

The Torch Parade Begins

Looking behind us, we can see nothing but an endless stream of flickering torches lighting up the night, as wide as the road and as far back as we can see.

Torch Parade On The Way to Manger Square

Torch Parade Coming to Manger Square

Many of us are in tears. This was so much more than any of us could have imagined. As Peter Ryan expressed in his journal later that night, "One of the greatest moments of my life!" For me and Nancy, and the other Pilgrims on our journey, we could all give a resounding "Amen!". Me and Nancy and our team of Pilgrims are overwhelmed with gratitude to God for making, after all our struggles and doubts, this "impossible" moment happen.

Nancy and Robin Arriving at Manger Square
With Our Caravan of Pilgrims

Thousands Gathered in Manger Square
Anticipating Our Arrival

Reaching Manger Square, there are thousands of people gathered there anticipating our arrival. Unfortunately, the Islamic prayer service blaring out of the loudspeaker from the back of the Square runs late—far too long actually—but eventually, the traditional Christmas Pageant begins.

Sami has arranged for a Christian dance troupe from Nazareth to present a dance reenactment of the traditional Christmas pageant. There is an expansive stage, with numerous spotlights, where a "cave" has been set up to represent where Jesus was born. The dancers twirl about the stage, acting out the story, starting with the angel's visit with the Shepherds, and continuing on to the Shepherds visit at the manger. Then, at the right time, our four Magi are led up onto the stage to present their gifts to the baby Jesus.

The Shepherds

The Angels

The Magi Presenting Their Gifts At The Manger

At the conclusion of the Christmas pageant performance, an announcement is made about our donation of 2000 olive tree saplings—a Christmas gift of peace to the Palestinian community—to help restore some of the 100's of olive groves that have been bulldozed by some Israeli settlers. Then the entire Pilgrim crew is invited up on stage. Our own Sami Awad, who has been acting as the M.C. for the entire evening, introduces us one by one to the cheering crowd.

Our Pilgrim Crew On Stage With Sami Awad

Following this, many family members of Palestinian martyrs (those killed in the months of violence) walk up onto the stage, their sorrow still visible, and warmly shake each of our hands.

Families of Those Killed in Bethlehem
Shaking our Hands

The Christmas 2000 celebration closes with our Andre Martinez and his mother, Gail, singing a poem written by Susan Lenzkes that Andre Martinez had put to music during our Journey—**He Comes in Winter**. The last verse concludes, "But He comes in winter, when hope lies frozen in the night, and blizzards wreak our souls. He comes, OUR LIVING HOPE!"

Andre Martinez on Stage
With His Mother, Prosper, and Tim McClelland

On Christmas morning Sami Awad had arranged for a local Palestinian family, with a 14 months old toddler, to receive our four Magi. Despite our traditional Christmas pageants suggesting that the Magi arrived at the time of Jesus' birth, Matthew Chapter 2, verse 11 tells us that they found the mother and child (toddler) in a house—not a manger—many months later. The image taken this morning, in a home similar to what would have been in Bethlehem near the time of Jesus' birth, serves as a fitting conclusion to our Pilgrimage.

Magi Presenting Gifts to Toddler

Reflecting on all that has occurred over the last three months to bring us to this amazing conclusion to our Pilgrimage for Peace, we recognize that we have been walking in a time of kairos—that is, a sacred window of time—when by God's grace all things are possible, according to His purposes.

ACKNOWLEDGEMENTS

We want to thank Phil and Norma Elkins for helping us in so many ways during the years we were seeking to set up our International Pilgrimage, and for all they did toward the end to locate our amazing team of International Pilgrims. We also want to thank David Bentley for his book, ***The 99 Beautiful Names of God, for all the people of the Book*** (William Carey Library, 1999). It was very important in providing our daily meditations every morning as we were traveling on the Journey. A special thanks to Jason Drake for his amazing color pictures for the book.

Also, we also want to give due thanks and much praise to the indigenous leaders throughout the Middle East who are largely responsible for our successful International Pilgrimage.

Dr. Riad Jarjour
Middle East Council of Churches,
who co-sponsored our Journey of the Magi 2000:
A Pilgrimage for Peace

General George Sada, Iraq

Rev. Nuhad Tomeh, Syria

Souhel Daas
Logistics in Syria and Jordan

Daoud Kuttab, Jordan

Jonathan Kuttab, Palestine

Sami Awad, Bethlehem
Leader of Holy Land Trust

THE CURRENT ACTIVITIES
OF HOLY LAND TRUST

Our goal from early on was to not only do the "impossible"—
our International Pilgrimage to honor Jesus on His 2000th
birthday—but to launch Holy Land Trust in Bethlehem to be
a vehicle to carry on the fight for peace and justice throughout
Bethlehem, Palestine, Israel and the Middle East.

To see the current ministries of Holy Land Trust, and to make
a contribution to their efforts, go to <u>https://holylandtrust.org</u>

Made in the USA
Columbia, SC
11 May 2022